Every Right for Every Child

Every Right for Every Child

Governance and Accountability

Editor

Enakshi Ganguly Thukral

Routledge
Taylor & Francis Group
LONDON   NEW YORK   NEW DELHI

First published 2011 in India
by Routledge
912 Tolstoy House, 15–17 Tolstoy Marg, Connaught Place, New Delhi 110 001

Simultaneously published in the UK
by Routledge
2 Park Square, Milton Park, Abingdon, Oxfordshire OX14 4RN

First issued in paperback 2015

Routledge is an imprint of the Taylor & Francis Group, an informa business

Typeset by
Bukprint India
B-180A, Guru Nanak Pura
Laxmi Nagar, Delhi 110 092

This volume is published in collaboration with HAQ Centre for Child Rights,
New Delhi.

British Library Cataloguing-in-Publication Data
A catalogue record of this book is available from the British Library

ISBN-13: 978-1-138-66000-7(pbk)
ISBN-13: 978-0-415-67837-7(hbk)

To all children, who teach us never to give up

Contents

List of Tables

List of Figures

Foreword

The year 2009 marked the twentieth anniversary of the adoption of the United Nations' Convention on the Rights of the Child (UNCRC). In the years since I was first engaged in the drafting of this very important convention, I have seen many significant changes occur. Not only is it the most ratified human rights treaty in the UN system, but a process of social change has taken place at the national level as a result. Indeed, laws, policies and discourse have changed across countries, and children are increasingly perceived as full-fledged citizens.

In spite of the important achievements made over the last 20 years, and significant experience that we have gained along the way, children's concerns continue to run the risk of being perceived as minor issues and are often placed in a growing waiting slot.

There is still a perception that policy decisions are neutral to children, and that the existing laws, policies and institution provide the necessary environment to protect children from any negative development. Promoting evidence-based approaches to overcome the many challenges that compromise children's development and well-being is an expression of wisdom and good economics. But it remains above all a question of accountability for the rights of the child.

The implementation of children's rights is intrinsically linked to strong political will. Information, analysis and knowledge constitute core building blocks of a system of public scrutiny and reporting on the rights of the child and the foundation of a transparent and accountable governance system. Indeed, these are the essential dimensions that enable governments to take the right decisions at the right time.

Governance systems must safeguard children's rights and ensure child protection from violence, abuse, exploitation and discrimination within families, the school, child institutions, and more broadly, society as a whole. Human rights standards provide a tangible indicator of how genuine national commitments are to respecting the human dignity of the child at all times; to addressing risk factors that compromise children's development and citizenship; to investing in the social inclusion of the most vulnerable; and to promoting actions that are built upon children's best interests, perspectives and experiences.

Partnering with children and listening to them is key. Joining hands with young people and listening to their views and experiences allows us to gain a better understanding of the hidden face of human rights violations, including any form of violence. More importantly, it helps us to become better equipped to prevent their occurrence, to develop better and more lasting strategies, and to monitor progress and impact achieved.

Organisations across the world have developed initiatives and methods to monitor state performance and accountability for children. They have engaged with their governments to make governance systems more responsive to the rights, well-being and concerns of children. They have worked towards the recognition of children's citizenship, empowering children to participate in decision-making and influence decisions for the improvement of their lives. This book attempts to bring together some of these initiatives. It enables us to gain an understanding of good governance for children and the realisation of their economic, cultural, social, civil and political rights.

These initiatives illustrate how our actions must be grounded in the principle of indivisibility of human rights and guided by the best interests of the child. Violation of children's rights undermines the enjoyment of all rights and has serious, life-long effects on children's lives and well-being. Violence undermines child development, learning abilities and school performance, inhibits positive relationships, produces trauma, low self-esteem and often leads to risk-taking and aggressive behaviour, and at times self-inflicted harm.

In these initial years of the twenty-first century, nations are challenged by many competing priorities, hard-pressed by the economic down turn, confronted with a serious food and environmental crisis and an increasing difficulty to secure funding and sustain investment.

At the same time, in countries in the north as well as the south there is a growing search and demand for child-centred solutions that help cushion children against the impact of the crisis and effectively safeguard their human rights. Knowledge lays the foundation for creativity, openness for change and confidence in investment in human development. With sound research, national planning and policy making can be strategically shaped, external relations influenced and mind-sets shifted in favour of the realisation of children's rights; and in this process children can and must be seriously perceived as indicators of social progress.

To consolidate good governance for children's rights, we need to focus on the holistic being of the child and move away from compartmentalised approaches and fragmented actions to more integrated and cross-sectoral interventions that are enriched by knowledge from diverse disciplines.

Let us capture the diverse changing nature of childhood and the dynamic and evolving agency of children—as citizens of today, rather than adults in the making.

Let us reflect on the achievements we have been able to promote and on the many challenges that prevail to ensure the universal realisation of children's rights. Informed by the experience we have gained across nations and inspired by the ideals of the Convention on the Rights of the Child, this is the time to renew our commitment to children's rights—not just as an evolving routine in our daily work, but by re-energising the world in an irresistible sense of urgency and ambition.

Marta Santos Pais

UN Special Representative of the UN Secretary-General on Violence against Children; former member of the UN Committee on the Rights of the Child and former Director of the UNICEF Innocenti Research Centre in Florence

Preface

This book has been in the making for over four years. It all began with the need for exploring the concept of good governance and children in the course of our work through our Children and Governance Programme at HAQ: Centre for Child Rights.

While creating and building tools for monitoring the state's performance, and using the results to hold it accountable for the gaps, we realised that we were not quite answering some of the bigger questions: What is good governance vis-à-vis children? What are the standards and indicators? Can there be one answer for this question that is applicable to all countries of the world?

We realised that while agencies and experts have attempted to define and lay out the parameters of good governance in general for all people, there was not enough data and analysis available when it came to linking it with children's rights in a cohesive and comprehensive manner. UNICEF and Save the Children, in a concept note for a meeting titled 'Governance: Good Enough for Children?' say that although the measures of implementation of the UN Convention on the Rights of the Child (UNCRC) point to an agenda for action, these have not secured a position of influence within either the discourse on or practice of good governance, nor has the child rights constituency tradition-ally engaged with the governance agenda.[1] Not sur-

---

[1] Concept note for 'Governance: Good Enough for Children? Meeting on children and governance as part of the celebrations of the twentieth anniversary of the adoption of the Convention on the Rights of the Child', organised by UNICEF and Save the Children on October 27, 2009, New York.

prisingly, 'issues such as corruption, taxation and the rule of law are rarely the focus of children's organisations, despite their relevance for the realisation of children's rights'.[2]

At the same time, there are organisations in many countries working on the issues of governance, monitoring and accountability. Many of them have used budget analysis to monitor the governments' policies and actions as well as to engage with them. Organisations in South Africa and Brazil have also trained children to undertake budget analysis and even advocate with the government. Several other organisations have trained children to be their own advocates and work with local self-governments, etc. Others have engaged with the issues through research or community mobilisation. It became critical to draw on the diverse and yet comprehensive body of knowledge that has developed over the years from these initiatives. This book is a result of that search.

The first chapter attempts to explore the concept of children and governance as well as the involvement of children in governance, and the tools and methods that have been adopted internationally and in India to monitor state performance. In other words, it provides the overall framework for the book. It also describes the activities and the tools being developed by HAQ in India.

The African Child Policy Forum (ACPF) has pioneered a methodology for the analysis of the concept of child-friendliness and a child-friendliness index to assess, score and rank the performance of all 52 governments in Africa in *The African Report on Child Wellbeing 2008: How Child-friendly are African Governments?* Child-friendliness is a manifestation of the political will of governments to make the maximum effort to realise children's rights and well-being. The chapter by Assefa Bequele discusses the methodology as well as the results. One of the most interesting

---

[2] Ibid.

conclusions that emerge from the report is that poverty cannot always be an excuse for non-performance of governments. The study by ACPF shows that a number of countries with low GDP per capita spend significantly more of their limited resources on education and health sectors than some other countries with higher GDP per capita. Policy problems concerning children seem to be the result of lethargy and neglect rather than poverty. The African Child Policy Forum has shared this report with different governments and they believe that such an approach provides context to issues, successes, failures and lessons, and generates a positive inter-country competitiveness. The report also generated interest among African governments because they no longer saw themselves in relation to Norway, Australia or Papua New Guinea, with whom they had little in common, but in relation to their neighbours and regional partners.

HAQ: Centre for Child Rights owes its genesis, in part, to the Yugoslav Child Rights Centre and its founder Nevena Vuckovic Sahovic, who went on to become a member of the UN Committee on the Rights of the Child (2003–09). The Centre has been attempting to ensure children's rights in governance since the mid-1990s. Nevena Vuckovic Sahovic's chapter, 'Measures to Implement the Convention on the Rights of the Child and Good Governance: The Case of Serbia', dwells on the efforts and challenges of bringing up children and ensuring their rights and dignity in the backdrop of the political and economic crisis of the 1990s following the break-up of Yugoslavia, the creation of Serbia, the general collapse of the value system, and the rise of xenophobia and intolerance in the region.

Enrique Vásquez, in his chapter, 'A Story of Neglect: Children in Peru's Public Budgets', highlights how Peru has been neglecting its poorer children using the argument of lack of resources. Tracking the flow of financial resources to different programmes targeted at children, and monitoring the allocation expenditure and number of children covered, Vásquez shows how poor planning, inefficiency, poor management and leakage affect the outcomes for children. In doing so, he shares the methodology that has been adopted in Peru to monitor government performance founded on four basic principles: efficacy, efficiency, equity and transparency. By tracking budget allocations, expenditure and coverage of children he shows how the government is violating basic principles and points out where the gaps are.

Despite promises of non-discrimination and affirmative action made by governments, there are some children who fall through the gaps. This is because children are not a homogeneous group and often, in planning and implementing for all children, those who are vulnerable and marginalised are neglected or even excluded. Anita Ghai, in her chapter, 'Pedagogy of Writing Disabled Children's Rights into Governance', argues that despite being included in international human rights instruments, such as the UN Convention on the Rights of the Child as well the UN Convention on the Rights of Persons with Disabilities, there is very little evidence to show that disabled children find centre stage in decisions made by governments, nor are they part of decisions that concern them. Clearly, when developing parameters for responsive or good governance in the context of children, special attention is needed for children with disabilities.

Drawing upon her long experience of working on elimination of child labour and the right to education in the MV Foundation in India, Shantha Sinha, in 'Overcoming Barriers for Getting Children Out of Work and into Schools', illustrates the role and importance of social mobilisation to both monitor government's performance and force it to act on behalf of children. She dwells on the complementary responsibilities of the state, non-government organisations (NGOs) and the community in the realisation of child rights. Non-government organisations can act through the process of social mobilisation so that local bodies can take a stand on abolishing child labour and putting the child in school, and through resolution of conflicts at the level of the family, employers and the school. This complex process involves building networks and appropriate norms at all levels.

The UN Convention on the Rights of the Child does not mention the term 'child participation' explicitly but the tone and tenor of its articles advocate a proactive role for children in matters concerning them, upholding an independent personality of the child. Article 12—one of the general principles of the CRC—articulates the real essence of the idea of children's participation. The chapters authored by Shaamela Casseim, Deborah Ewing and Mabusi Kgwete, Margarida Maria Marques and Kavita Ratna are part of the discourse on children *in* governance. They show how children can be part of governance, and actively participate in budget monitoring and advocacy as well as local self-governance.

Kavita Ratna, in 'Children's Impact on State Governance: Overarching Issues', unpacks the whole concept of child participation and child protaganism in the context of every child's right to be heard and be part of decisions that concern her/him. Through her chapter and drawing on her work with children in Concerned for Working Children and Bhima Sangha, the children's group, she takes the current discussions on child participation, citizenship and protaganism to the next level. She argues for the right to self-determination of children as the foundation of the rights discourse. According to her, for the right to self-determination to be exercised most effectively, there is a need for protagonism that either leads to or is a result of 'empowerment' which ensures 'mutual' accountability between the rights holders and the duty bearers. The children's participation should embody processes that empower them to negotiate with the duty bearers. This is true of any meaningful protagonism and applies to children as well.

The Institute for Democracy in South Africa (IDASA) was one of the first organisations in the world to undertake budget analysis from a child rights' perspective and engage children in the process, as has been done by the Centre for the Defence of Children and Adolescents (Cedeca-Ceará) in Brazil. Their initiatives and learnings can be models to organisations and countries across the world. Since 1995 the Children's Budget Unit (CBU), based in Cape Town, has been using national and provincial government budgets as monitoring mechanisms to advance child-specific socioeconomic rights. During the first five years, the main effort centred on tracking budget allocations and programmes intended to reach children, and highlighting challenges regarding delivery of services. *Are Poor Children being Put First? Child Poverty and the Budget* was published in 2000 (Casseim et al. 2000). From 2001 onwards (with the publication of *Budgeting for Child Socio-Economic Rights—Government Obligations and the Child's Right to Social Security and Education* [Casseim and Streak 2002]), significant effort was made in analysing the legal framework that ensures social and economic child rights in South Africa, and linking this framework to budget analysis. This methodology combined a variety of legal obligations, socioeconomic indicators, budget information, and an analysis of governmental programme conceptualisation, design and impact. *Using Government Budgets as a Monitoring Tool* (Kgamphe 2004) was published in 2004.

Shaamela Casseim, Deborah Ewing and Mabusi Kgwete were all part of IDASA's Child Budget Unit in Cape Town, which has since closed. South Africa has a longer history of children's participation than the UNCRC, even longer than the age of the country that began during the anti-apartheid struggle. Their chapter, '"Everywhere We Go, Our Presence is Felt": Reflections on a Governance and Budget-monitoring Project in South Africa', contributes to a body of knowledge of the experiences of children preparing to monitor their local government budget and service delivery and is located in a theoretical framework of 'rights', 'citizenship' and 'participation'. It shares the methodology adopted, the challenges and the learnings from the Children Participating in Governance (CPG) project. Negotiating through societal and administrative pressures, the authors share how they had to ensure that children participated without jeopardising their other rights, and ensure the children's physical security and comfort, as well as protect their dignity and emotional well-being. They conclude that advocating for children's active citizenship and their participation requires more than opening spaces for children in the decision-making process. Children's citizenship participation requires a change in the processes of participation and increasing the knowledge and abilities of children. Most importantly, there is a need to change adult spaces of decision-making so that they enable citizenship participation and create public political spaces for children, persons with disabilities, women, illiterate persons, excluded people, people living in poverty and people living outside of cities. Continued and meaningful children's participation requires consistent and sustained support. In the case of South Africa, the CPG project ended as IDASA moved its Children's Budget Unit out of Cape Town and the project managers left.

Founded in 1994, the Centre for the Defence of Children and Adolescents (Cedeca-Ceará), initiated its programme of monitoring the Fortaleza city budget. This was done from the understanding that the struggle for the human rights of children and young people has to be conducted through discussions of public policies that directly affect these rights, by being informed about the allocation of public resources to implement those policies, and through social control in the allocation and spending of public resources. A follow-up project in 2002–03, with the support of Cordaid Netherlands and Save the Children Sweden, attempted to create a methodology to empower the young to intervene and participate in public policies through budgetary legislation.

Margarida Maria Marques, in her chapter, 'To Guarantee Public Investments in Order to Effect Rights: Monitoring of the Public Budget with the Participation of Adolescents— The Experience of Cedeca-Ceará', describes the experience of monitoring the public budget, particularly in the area of infancy, an analysis developed by Cedeca-Ceará, and with the participation of adolescents in the whole process. This experience takes place in Fortaleza, capital of the state of Ceará, Brazil. The issues raised in the chapter are fundamentally about the social control of the state and the right of participation of children and adolescents with a reflection upon the role of the state and the society in the process of 'invisibilisation' of infancy. It also discusses the contradictions between the improvements reached in the institutional area and in the effectiveness of the law, particularly regarding the guarantee of children and adolescents' rights.

In July 2009, HAQ, in an effort to explore the concept of good governance for children, organised an international colloquium on 'Children and Governance: Holding the State Accountable' which brought together participants from countries of South Asia, Africa and the UK. This book also draws upon some of the discussions from the colloquium.

Clearly, an understanding of good governance with respect to children is about the recognition and acceptance of children as citizens in their own right, therefore as rights holders. Despite some acknowledgement over the years, this still remains the greatest challenge. Children continue to be viewed as extensions of adults or simply as members of families and communities both by planners as well as the families themselves. Unless child rights becomes an indicator of development and mainstreaming of children's rights a part of any planning in the country, whatever it may be for, governance cannot be child-friendly or child-responsive. Simply speaking, when we build our roads, do we ensure that they are safe for children to walk and cycle on? Are the footpaths at a height that even the youngest child can climb on to and walk? At a macro level, do the agricultural policies push more and more children into malnutrition or make them healthy and food secure? Do the development policies leading to displacement also see how they affect children, making them more vulnerable to abuse and exploitation? These are only a few examples of how every policy of the government can be scanned through the child rights lens.

It is hoped that this book will contribute to a greater understanding of what is a critical assessment of state performance (shining the spotlight on the continuing disempowerment of many sections of children); self-monitoring systems for the state (safeguards and systemic checks and balances to ensure that policies and programmes do not endanger children's interests); the role of legal instruments and the relevance of international agreements and state compliance to them; and the role of diverse groups like NGOs, elected representatives and activists, among others.

Acknowledgements

For me, this book has been in the making for what seems like forever. Indeed, at one stage, I felt that it will never get to the printing press. The authors that are finally included in this volume are not the ones who had initially confirmed, leading to ulcers and heartache as they kept dropping out. I am therefore grateful to all the contributors, the ones who have been with this project from the very beginning as well as those who agreed to join in later.

Putting together any international collection—over different languages and different time zones— is not easy. It is true, unlike in the old days when I had edited my earlier book communicating by 'snail mail', the entry of e-mail has made communication easy, but it has also made life more complicated; we expect and demand instant responses. So I thank all the authors for their patience with my constant barrage of endless e-mail exchanges.

On the lighter side, to Margarida Marques from Brazil I owe the knowledge of the use of the Google translator that enabled us to communicate with each other and we both thank Google which enabled us to communicate since I know no Portuguese and she, very little English.

Manisha Priyam walked into my office one day, and in the course of the conversation offered to help with Shantha Sinha's chapter, since by the time the chapter was getting finalised, Shantha had become the Chairperson of the National Commission for Protection of Child Rights, and her time was at a premium. Manisha's assistance was very welcome.

My team at office has had to bear with my sighs of disappointment as well as squeals of delight as the book progressed, especially my co-director Bharti Ali who shares my room and has dealt with my highs and lows over the last four long years, in her usual stoic manner.

I thank Prava Rai for copy-editing the manuscript for submission to Routledge and Paromita Shastri for her initial editorial inputs.

And most of all it is my family—Kishore, my spouse, and Shiuli and Atish—my children, who have to bear with me, struggling, crying or laughing. But them, I will continue to take for granted, as I do my parents, Pratima and S. P. Ganguly and my sister, Meenakshi. They are my pillars and they better never move.

1

Children and Governance:
Concept and Practice

Enakshi Ganguly Thukral

Meenal is a bright-eyed Indian girl from north-west India. She is intelligent, smart and out-going. Pulled out of school by her father, and put to work filling salties into plastic bags for eight hours a day, did not deter her or kill her spirit. After all, being the eldest of her five siblings, it was her duty to support the family and she did what was expected of her. Neither she, nor her parents, nor the society she lived in asked the question, 'What about her?' The school system in her town did not pull her in to ensure that she got her right to education and childhood. At some point she came in touch with an organisation that worked with children in her town. It promoted children's forums and encouraged them to exercise their right to participation. Bright and intelligent, it was no surprise that Meenal soon became not only active in the group, but one of its leaders. She participated in meetings and jamborees organised for children across the country, even met the president of India, got selected by children from all over the country to represent them at an international meet and she travelled abroad, getting on to a plane and flying to the other end of the world, to a country she probably did not even know existed. Her first and perhaps her last journey on an airplane was exciting and exhilarating; although the free cokes and abundance of food made her totally sick.

Meenal returned from meeting people from across the world, participating in workshops, addressing meetings on rights of children, picking up a smattering of Spanish,

Portuguese and English, eating food that she had never eaten before, only to find her self working in a diamond factory, polishing minute diamonds. And yet neither she nor any one around her asked why she was still barely literate and whether this was not a violation of her rights. The organisation with which she was associated said that since she was now over 14 years of age, there was little that they could do, except emotionally support her.[1] The family began to pressurise her to get married. Beautiful as she was, proposals were not a problem. Here she put her foot down and resisted. Her experience of being a leader of the children's group was very helpful and she had support from them. As she got older, she fell in love with a boy, but as soon as she turned 18, her parents married her off to a man they chose, ignoring her own choice. After all, she was the eldest child in the family. She must not do anything to bring 'shame' upon it, and she caved in.

Is Meenal happy? Who knows? After all, despite having attended several workshops on child rights, and having promoted it through her organisation, in her personal life, she has never had the right to exercise them; nor has the state, the government, the system which is obligated to protect her rights intervened.

What does Meenal's story illustrate about governance and children? More importantly, where does it leave a child like Meenal, who is aware of her rights and duties, but the system of governance has not created an environment wherein she can her exercise rights? It is in the context of children like Meenal that we need to discuss governance and children in India and elsewhere in the world.

Children, Citizenship and Governance

Governance and the realisation of rights of children are intrinsically connected. However, despite it being increasingly recognised across the world that improved or 'good' governance is a precondition for sustained poverty reduction and a peaceful and stable society, and being a term that is frequently used by civil society groups, governments and aid agencies at all levels, it is seldom discussed in the context of children. As Sheridan Bartlett points out,

> even progressive governments that refer carefully in their policies to 'women and men', may express an unwitting bias against children. This is not unique to government. This bias can run deep in many quarters. Even in discussions among committed development professionals who are fully aware of the benefits of taking gender into account, it is not uncommon for interest to fade if the topic of children comes up. The unspoken message is that bringing children into the discussion is a not-quite-relevant tangent—that surely their needs are met if their parents' needs are met. To some degree, this is true. But it is also true that boys and girls of different ages experience the world in particular ways, and may be affected in particular ways (sometimes profound and long-lasting) by a range of decisions and actions. (2005: 3)

Children's rights even today stand at the same crossroads that women's issues did two-and-a-half decades ago. At best they are seen as ornamental, and an add-on to the more 'real problems of society'. They are relegated to the realm of touchy-feely sentimental 'good work' that children need. Children's rights are not seen to be political and mainstream. Often even those put in charge of implementing children's rights do not see it as 'real developmental work' or 'real governance work' unlike defence, infrastructure or commerce. Needless to say initiatives for children are presented almost as a cosmetic addition to the 'real' work of local government, rather than as part of an integrated response that makes children and youth a more visible component of this real work.

Hence, while governance with respect to citizens of any country as a whole has been discussed since the inception of the concept of state, it is nascent in its conceptualisation with reference to children. That is because children have been, and even now continue to be viewed as extensions of adults rather than as citizens in their own right.

The reality is that children are citizens the minute they are born and entitled to as much attention, if not more given their age and vulnerability. Investing in them is as critical in their own interest, as it is in the interest of society. The challenge is that children are unable to demand or exercise their rights and need the recognition and support of adults. The second and perhaps an equally important challenge as well as opportunity is that children grow up, so their status changes. As they grow, they need age-specific inputs. Once they become adults, they will behave and respond to others exactly as they have been responded to as children. They are citizens of today and also adults of tomorrow. And society will reap tomorrow as it sows today.

Clearly, governance begins with recognition of entitlements and citizenship. People do not suddenly become citizens on reaching a certain age. Legal age definitions are arbitrary, and do not reflect the range of capacities of children and adolescents. Human capacities develop and change throughout life at different rates according to individual potential and social environment. They vary from child to child and depend on the contexts they grow up in, on children's mental development (see Article 23 of the Convention on Rights of the Child [CRC]), and their social, economic, cultural and religious background. Citizenship must be learned through everyday experiences of family and community life, education, civic and political awareness. Access to opportunities in school, media, sports and culture is critical for developing and practicing citizenship skills (Inter-Agency Working Group on Children's Participation 2008: 5).

Citizenship represents the collection of rights and obligations that define the members of a community. These rights and obligations encompass legal empowerment and justice, political participation and decision-making, social engagement, economic rights and access to resources. Citizenship has two complementary aspects: citizenship rights and citizenship practice. Citizenship includes notions of rights and responsibilities, status and practice, individual and community. Western cultures tend to emphasise individual rights, whereas Asian societies emphasise the responsibilities of the individual towards family, community and society. In order to thrive, societies require a combination of the two (Inter-Agency Working Group on Children's Participation 2008: 3). The citizenship rights of any individual, including children, include civil, political, social, cultural and economic rights. Civil and political rights are people's entitlements to liberty and equality, and include the rights to freedom of expression and religion, to take part in political life that is appropriate for their age, and to have access to information, skills and opportunities for development and enhanced participation. The civil right to equality is expressed in the right to equal protection to redress if injured by another person and to a fair investigation and trial if suspected of a crime. In some countries, citizenship can also mean 'nationality' or the membership of a nation state. However, citizenship and nationality are not synonymous. Human rights law does not categorically obligate governments to extend nationality to all residents (ibid.).

If access to rights is restricted to children who only have name and nationality, many children across the world who are fleeing their countries with their parents due to conflicts or economic distress, etc. or who are born of parents who have migrated will be denied protection. It is here that the definition of citizenship that recognises foreigners and stateless persons who are in the country on legal grounds and are able to enjoy the same rights and freedoms and also bear the same duties as citizens, becomes important. Such a presumption of citizenship is a unique child protection provision, which serves to support children affected by conflicts (Duncan 2008). Clearly, a child must be protected and all his/her rights realised wherever he/she is, and this recognition and realisation of rights must not be constrained by boundaries of countries, especially in a world such as the one in which we live today where huge populations are being displaced and forced to move across political boundaries.

A commonly accepted definition of governance is the way the state exercises its political, economic and administrative power. Key attributes of good governance are that institutions and processes are built on the rule of law, accountability, openness, effectiveness and responsiveness and space for equal and meaningful participation to all sections of the society irrespective of caste, creed, religion, class, culture and age group (Abdellatif 2003). This kind of governance would, thus, necessarily be based on a rights-based approach towards its citizenry. Although the term generally refers to the actions undertaken by governments, it is also understood to go beyond government and to include the relationships between formal government institutions and an active civil society. 'Rather than government taking decisions in isolation', explains Diana Mitlin, 'there is a growing acceptance (indeed expectation) of an engaged state negotiating its policies and practices with those who are a party to, or otherwise affected by, its decisions' (Mitlin 2004: 1).

It is only with the adoption of the United Nation's Convention on the Rights of the Child that children's human rights came to be recognised or even addressed separately, based on the recognition of citizenship rights of children. Indeed, it would not be wrong to state that it is also with the requirement of reporting on the general measures of implementation as part of the countries' reports to the UN

Committee that special attention began to be paid to governance for children. Although most societies may have informal mechanisms for children's participation, the recognition of children's own agency and their right to be heard in decisions concerning them came to be openly discussed and addressed following the UNCRC.

This brings us to two concepts that need to be examined as far as children as citizens are concerned—children *and* governance and children *in* governance.

Children *and* governance involves developing an understanding and engagement with the systems of governance that ensure the realisation of the rights of the child. This may not necessarily include the 'protaganism' of children. Interested adults in society may choose to work on ensuring systems of governance by working towards creating the system, implementing programmes, or through research, advocacy or training.

Children *in* governance, on the other hand, requires building partnerships with the children themselves participating in governance and recognises that children are 'agents of change'.

> Children's citizenship and governance is concerned with the active participation of girls, boys and young people in the familial, social, economic, political and cultural arenas. It is a step-by-step process through which they develop the skills, understanding and values to influence decision-making and outcomes at local, national and international levels in an environment that recognises them as competent social actors. (Save the Children 2003 and 2004)

This is only possible through the recognition of their right to participation.

> The right to participate in decisions made on their behalf is one of the bundles of civil and political rights provided in the CRC that are usually associated with

liberal democracies. Because of their immaturity, children may need extra assistance in order to be able to exercise these rights, assistance that should be provided by duty-bearers. (Ennew et al. 2004)

However, as was remarked by the UN Special Rapporteur on Human Rights and Youth in 1991, dialogue between adults and children is limited because of the absence of structures through which children can 'filter their opinions through to decision-making bodies' (Van Bueren 1995: 13). In other words, children's roles as protagonists are dependent on spaces that are created, or not created, for them by the state or the adults in society. How then does the state respond to the concerns of children? Are the state mechanisms adequately equipped for it? What are the characteristics of a child-friendly governance system?

Children and Governance

Children and governance is essentially about the recognition of children as citizens in their own right, therefore, as rights holders. Fundamental to this recognition is state action by formulating legislation, policies and programmes and also through the systems it sets up to implement them—the executive, legislature and judiciary. It has been recognised that improved or 'good' governance, based on a rights-based approach, is a precondition for sustained poverty reduction and a peaceful and stable society.[2] By ratifying the UNCRC, 191 countries, including India, have agreed to ensure implementation of children's rights. According to Save the Children, 'Governance involves structures and systems. It is concerned with power and resources and opportunities to influence matters that affect individuals and their communities. For children and young people, governance relates to several contexts such as family, school governance and national and international governance' (Save the Children 2003 and 2004).

Governments are obligated to fulfilling the rights of children, as well as playing regulatory and supervisory roles to ensure non-state actors' compliance with child rights codes. In general, child rights impose three distinct obligations on governments: the obligations to *respect*, *protect* and *fulfill* those rights.[3] As was remarked by Shantha Sinha, chairperson of the National Commission for the Protection of Child Rights, India,

> It must be recognised unequivocally by all that it is the State alone that is the rightful agency to protect children's rights and their well-being. We do recognise that for many marginalised children, there is a distinct deficit of childhood and citizenship and that this is primarily due to a deficit in State policy and planning. Democracy means justice, freedom and equity. We must enhance the meaning of democracy in order to highlight our children's rights. (HAQ 2009)

The obligation to respect child rights requires governments to refrain from interfering directly or indirectly with children's enjoyment of their rights. The obligation to protect children against abuse and exploitation refers to the governments' duty to prevent, investigate, punish and ensure redress for the harm caused by abuses of their rights by third parties, such as private individuals or other non-state actors. The obligation to fulfil these rights necessitates that governments fulfil the rights of children, through the implementation of legislative, administrative, adequate and appropriate budgetary, judicial and other measures. Additionally, the obligation to fulfil child rights refers to the progressive realisation of rights, and includes governments' duties to facilitate and provide for basic needs, particularly when children's families are unable to do so (ibid.).

Governance with respect to children in this fast-changing world needs to keep pace and be responsive to the changing needs of children, which have been referred to as 'Newly Emerging Needs' by Oudenhoven and Wazir. They recommend that policy makers must be sensitive, flexible and increasingly prepared for new and as yet unfamiliar situations that we are constantly confronted with in a fast-changing world. They warn against a 'cookie cutter' approach to developing interventions. For example, globalisation and increasing commercialisation of lifestyles, growing use of new technologies, the challenges posed by information technology, environmental degradation and pollution lie at the root of needs that were not so evident two decades ago (impact of HIV/AIDS, tsunami, increasing numbers of forced evictions, more cases of juvenile diabetes and even obesity are some examples) (Oudenhoven and Wazir 2006: 23, 26, 31). At the same time, just as children's needs keep changing, they vary in different countries, or in different locations within the same country, according to urban, rural or regional contexts. The children also differ and change according to age and sex. It is often argued that the diverse needs of children based on age, gender and other differences make it difficult to plan. The counter argument is that it is critical to acknowledge these differences and yet address them if rights of all children are to be realised.

Good governance related to rights of the child, as with any other category of citizens of a country, is measurable by the level of realisation of rights: existence of relevant laws and policies, number of children enrolled into schools, number of children immunised, number of children placed in institutions or number of children using harmful substances. It is hard to imagine that achieving a high level of exercise of child rights is possible within a governance system that is non-transparent, disorganised, corrupt and non-accountable. In other words, child rights can be best realised when the state provides for a high level of participation, equality, the rule of law and efficiency (Sahovic in Chapter 3 in this book).

The innovative initiative of the government of Bhutan to measure gross national happiness of its citizens, including children, is worth examining. This approach to governance clearly goes beyond formulation of laws, policies and programmes and implementing them. In using this approach, the government is acknowledging its responsibility of ensuring that the citizens are indeed content with the initiatives and measures taken by the government for them. The government sees its obligation beyond the action of 'providing and provisioning' of the realisation of rights. It is also concerned about the impact of state action towards the promotion and fulfilment of their well-being, leading to its citizens' happiness.

This brings us to the need for holding the state accountable for its actions and inactions. Accountability is a distinctive, complex and central feature of human rights, and is concerned with the requirement of the state to fully comply with its obligations—national, regional or international. This involves continuous monitoring by government and civil society. Just as rights holders have the right to receive information on whether governments are fulfilling their obligations, governments have the obligation to make public all available information on its programmes, policies, laws and budgets. Examples of individuals and groups seeking accountability show that the real challenge is to convert legal commitments into specific measures of implementation (Potts undated).

The key to measuring good governance is:
- Monitoring its performance, and
- Holding it accountable for its actions.

This includes:
- Financial accountability, which is about allocation, disbursement and utilisation of funds.
- Performance accountability, which is about demonstrating and accounting for performance through implementation of initiatives in the light of agreed indicators—the focus being service, output and outcome or result.

- Political or democratic accountability involves policy making, political process and elections. (Brinkerhoff 2003)

Unfortunately, despite many organisations working all over the world for many years on issues concerning children, it is only now that the connection between children and good governance is beginning to be explored. HAQ: Centre for Child Rights, Delhi is one of the organisations trying to do so in a systematic manner, and as was pointed out by the participants, the colloquium organised in July 2009 was perhaps the first one of its kind in the world to discuss this issue (HAQ 2009).

> Ensuring accountability on the road towards universal access involves a number of things. It means monitoring Governments' steps aimed at progressive realisation of these rights and highlighting any failure to do so. It means holding Governments accountable for obligations of immediate effect, for example where scaling up access discriminates a certain group such as children ... it involves providing the framework, mechanisms and environment for holding officials accountable, including ensuring freedom of speech, accessible justice, transparent government (including transparent budget processes), the ability of civil society to organise and safety of activists to hold Governments to account.
>
> *Louise Arbour, United Nations high commissioner for human rights, statement on the occasion of World AIDS Day, December 1, 2006*

Violations of rights take place both by acts of omission and commission. An act of violence or withdrawal of a basic service is an act of commission, but non-provision of resources, which includes budgetary provisions and services, is an act of omission. With the recognition of the relationship between governance and child rights, several groups across the world, as well as governments themselves have been initiating actions and setting mechanisms in place to ensure child-sensitive governance. Several groups have also initiated mechanisms to monitor state accountability in the realisation of child rights.

The basis of any work on children and governance must be the human rights principles that lay down the role of the state as the primary duty bearer, accountable for the realisation of all rights held by its people—children, women and men. However, for it to be truly sustainable, there is an urgent need to mainstream children's rights into all developmental efforts (just as gender mainstreaming has come to be recognised)—governmental and non-governmental.

This means, unless all government policies and actions, be it the agricultural policy, the drug policy, policy on displacement and rehabilitation, forest laws, mining policy, and the like, are examined through a child's rights lense, any attempt to address violation or denial of children's rights will stand defeated, leaving scope for more and more children to fall out of the social security and safety net. A very good example of this is the National Programme of Action for Children in South Africa (NPA), which was envisaged as an instrument for ensuring that poor children are 'put first' in policy, government budgets and service delivery. In putting children first in government's budgets the NPA called upon every department to give priority to children's needs in every decision about how to spend public funds, thereby ensuring the 'mainstreaming of children's needs into all budget decisions' (Casseim et al. 2000: vii).

> The concept of mainstreaming means that each government department incorporates children's issues into their respective portfolios. It calls upon each department to reflect its commitment to children, with corresponding budgetary allocation. With this approach, there is no single 'children's budget', rather, children's issues . . . (are supposed to) . . . inform every department's budget. (Government of South Africa 1999: 9)

At the same time, it is well recognised that children in any country are not a homogeneous group, and their needs would differ according to age, gender, ethnicity, socioeconomic status and physical and mental capacity. Additionally, even while there are specific age, gender and ability-appropriate interventions required for children, there is also a critical need to ensure that all children have all rights.

Holding the State Accountable

The example of HAQ: Centre for Child Rights in India over the last 11 years is an example of work on all three of the initiatives mentioned in the last paragraph. The core of the organisation's work is developing tools for monitoring state response and holding it accountable for its omissions and commissions in the realisation of child rights. Financial monitoring is done through its Budget for Children (BfC) analysis and performance monitoring through its status of children reports (HAQ 2002, 2005 and 2008). HAQ undertakes political and democratic accountability through its monitoring and analysis of parliamentary questions.

Monitoring of state performance is complimented with its advocacy initiatives for policy and law change based on the insights it gains through direct intervention to help protect children through legal assistance and counselling services. Training and capacity-building of administrators, such as the police, the judiciary, teachers, counsellors, district- and state-level officials and those responsible for implementing the Juvenile Justice Act and other laws and programmes supports the implementation of initiatives for children.

◊

Financial Monitoring and Accountability

Over the years, it has been widely recognised by groups across the world, and India, that regular analysis and monitoring of the budget provides a critical value addition to public advocacy initiatives. The budget showcases the government's true priorities vis-à-vis planned expenditure and is the most solid and articulate expression of the government's priorities, performances, decisions and intentions.

> At the beginning of each (financial) year, (the) budget is the most important document, as resources have to be raised to the extent indicated therein and these are to be applied for the desired purposes indicated in the budget. When, however, the financial year is over, the accounts reflect the actual implementation of the financial planning . . . the figures speak for themselves, much more than verbose explanations. (Ganguly 2000: 5)

Hence, the budget is perhaps the most important policy document and has profound effects on its citizens.

Therefore, analysing government budgets helps civil society organisations to understand what is planned and where the gaps and the greatest needs exist. It enables groups and individuals to gain a realistic understanding of the political commitments of the government to a sector, a group of people or an issue. It also helps to ensure that budgets are transparent and accessible for the public. Such an analysis can also be used to challenge corruption and imbalances in resource allocation. Based on this, evidence-based advocacy strategies can be developed to ensure government accountability and impel duty-bearers to make the necessary changes to ensure that the rights of their citizens are protected.

Realisation of rights of children requires financial commitment that matches the commitments made to children through the constitution, laws, policies and programmes and the ratification of international instruments. Article 4 of the UN Convention of the Rights of the Child imposes on states to invest the maximum available resources.

Expanding on this the UN Committee on the Rights of the Child has in General Comment 5 drawn upon the Convention on Economic, Social and Cultural Rights in asserting that 'even where the available resources are demonstrably inadequate, the obligation remains for a State party to strive to ensure the widest possible enjoyment of the relevant rights under the prevailing circumstances ...' Whatever their economic circumstances, states are required to undertake all possible measures towards the realisation of the rights of the child, paying special attention to the most disadvantaged groups. Recognising the implications of economic change on children it also states, '...the Committee has been deeply concerned by the often negative effects on children of structural adjustment programmes and transition to a market economy. The implementation duties of article 4 and other provisions of the Convention demand rigorous monitoring of the effects of such changes and adjustment of policies to protect children's economic, social and cultural rights.'[4]

Despite laws and policies and as many as 122 programmes (the numbers have since changed) and schemes directed at children in 2000, there was very little change visible in the status of children who comprised almost one-third of the population. Time and again those concerned with children were told, the situation is grave, but the resources are limited. That was indeed the crux. What were the resources being invested by the government for children? Were they adequate? How did they match the outcomes in terms of indicators for children? In the wider context of poverty, disease, malnutrition, high mortality and increase in the number of children coming into conflict with the law, can neglect of children's health, development and protection requirements in financial terms be justified?

India had ratified the UN Convention of the Rights of the Child in 1992 and on March 19, 1997, India submitted its first report to the UN Committee on the Rights of the

Child. The Committee's Concluding Observations made in 2000 stressed on the need for the state party to take all necessary measures, including allocation of required resources (i.e., human and financial) and ensure appropriate distribution of resources at the central, state and local levels, and where needed, within the framework of international cooperation (UN Committee on the Rights of Child 2000).

Budget analysis fits perfectly into HAQ's work of watching over and monitoring state performance in all matters pertaining to the realisation of child rights. While such initiatives in budget analysis were already being undertaken in India with respect to Dalits, tribal and rural development, etc, the focus on children was missing from any such analysis.

Released on September 11, 2001, HAQ's work on the Budget for Children (BfC) was the first endeavour of its kind in the country.[5] It highlighted the need for such analysis and set the initial direction for developing a methodology to do this more effectively. Since then, HAQ has been undertaking BfC analysis every year. Most laws and programmes in India are implemented by the states in India. Therefore, recognising that any understanding of children and budgets would remain incomplete without undertaking child budget work in the states, in 2002 HAQ decided to undertake BfC work in three sample states, extending it to six states in the next phase.

A budget for children is not a separate budget. It is merely an attempt to disaggregate those allocations made specifically for programmes that benefit children from the overall allocations made. This enables us to assess how far the policy and programme commitments are translated into financial commitments. This would also indicate political commitment of the government towards its young citizens.

Over the years, budget for children analysis or child budgeting, has come to be recognised as an empirical tool for not only monitoring state performance and holding the state accountable but also for child rights policy planning and programming. It has led to institutionalisation of child budgeting within the government through its inclusion in the National Plan of Action for Children, 2005 and the Eleventh Five Year Plan document (Government of India 2008). The final recognition of child budgeting, however, came only when the finance minister announced a separate statement on children when he presented the Finance Bill in parliament in 2008.

What is more, it was the government's acknowledgement of low allocation for the protection sector that led to the formulation of a comprehensive programme on child protection and the inclusion of a child budget in the Eleventh Five Year Plan document (Government of India 2008).

We will score another 'first' this year. A statement on child related schemes is included in the budget documents and Honourable Members will be happy to note that the total expenditure on these schemes is of the order of Rs. 33,434 crore.

P. Chidambaram, Finance Minister
Budget 2008–09

Recognising that children under 18 constitute a significant percentage of the Indian population, the Government is committed to their welfare and development. This statement reflects budget provisions of schemes that are meant substantially for the welfare of children. These provisions indicate educational outlays, provisions for the girl child, health, provisions for Child protection, etc.

Statement No. 22, Budget Provisions for Schemes for the Welfare of Children.

Expenditure Budget. Volume I,
Budget 2008–09

While most groups who undertake budget monitoring concentrate on budgets for the realisation of Economic Cultural and Social Rights (ESCR), HAQ believes that it is ESCR as well as civil and political rights that need to be monitored. That is why implementation of juvenile justice is a critical part of HAQ's work.

When India presented its second (first periodic report) to the UN Committee on the Rights of the Child in 2004 (Department of Women and Child Development 2004), the alternative report by the NGOs (India Alliance on Child Rights 2003), as well the briefing submissions made to the members contained a section on budgets for children. The Committee took serious note of that and made a strong recommendation in its Concluding Observations wherein it stated,

> While noting the efforts undertaken to increase the budget allocation for some social services, the Committee is concerned at the slow increase of the budget allocations for education and at the stagnation or even the decrease of expenses allocated to other social services. The Committee recommends that the State party: (a) Make every effort to increase the proportion of the budget allocated to the realization of children's rights to the 'maximum extent...of available resources' and, in this context, to ensure the provision, including through international cooperation, of appropriate human resources and to guarantee that the implementation of policies relating to social services provided to children remain a priority; and (b) Develop ways to assess the impact of budgetary allocations on the implementation of children's rights, and to collect and disseminate information in this regard. (UN Committee on the Rights of the Child 2004)

However, it must be remembered that budget analysis is only one of the tools for monitoring government performance and ensuring state accountability. It cannot be the only tool. State accountability can be determined best by juxtaposing budgetary allocations or 'inputs' against the 'outcomes' achieved in terms of actual benefits and access to services for which budgets have been allocated. BfC analysis can be turned into a more effective advocacy tool when it is combined with other initiatives. Towards this end, HAQ brings out status reports on children in the country (HAQ 2002, 2005 and 2008), which monitor the government's performance.

◊

Performance Accountability

If the laws, policies and budget-related priorities are to change in India in favour of children's rights, it is our legislators and parliamentarians who need to be influenced, and who require a greater understanding of what the country's children need. The question is: Are the MLAs and MPs in the country child-friendly enough? Who, among these, can we advocate to and work with? Analysing parliamentary questions and debates, and the production of a document such as 'Says a Child . . . Who Speaks for My Rights?' can be useful. While the more perceptive and enterprising among our MPs can use this document for critical self-reflection and performance, child-rights activists can use it for better advocacy.

Monitoring the judiciary is important. However, experience shows that the most effective way to do so is for organisations to engage with the judiciary through providing legal aid to children. This enables in the monitoring of its functioning through the scanning of the judgements and observing of court processes.

State accountability refers to the processes, norms and structures that require powerful actors (governors) to answer for their actions to another actor (the governed and/ or international community), and suffer some sanction if the performance is judged to be below standard. The aim of holding states accountable is to persuade governments to acknowledge their accountability to their own citizens and as well as the international community for violations of human rights through mechanisms such as reporting and petition (Sheahan 2009).

The success of governance has to do with whether or not children figure in the election manifestoes of politicians and their parties; whether or not they are at the heart of the budgeting process and are given a hearing; whether or not laws are based on the principle of the best interest of the child; whether or not the state has established a child-sensitive juvenile justice system; and whether or not we are moving towards a polity and society that is child-friendly. In other words, good governance means: politics that put children first, laws that protect them, and budgets that provide for them (Bequele 2009).

State action has to be monitored through well-tested methodology that provides empirical and verifiable results and thereupon held accountable for the commissions and omissions in its actions, in the realisation of civil and political rights as well as economic, cultural and social rights of all children, especially the most vulnerable and marginalised.

Children *in* Governance

The right to participation of people, of which universal adult franchise is one such avenue, has been recognised for adults for many decades. Traditionally, the family and community have sought their participation in earning for the family, participating in agricultural activities, undertaking household chores, family trade and vocation, but almost never in decision-making. But there have also been some formal mechanisms for building children's leadership skills and enlisting their participation through their involvement in Scouts and Guides, appointment as class representatives or monitors, representatives to student's councils in schools and later to students' unions in colleges and universities (Singh and Karkara 2002).

However, the important question is whether children themselves can exercise or demand for the realisation of their own rights or whether this responsibility is to be undertaken on their behalf by adults—parents or other carers—and how decisions are made in their best interest (Lansdown 2009).

There is no one universally accepted definition of child participation. Child participation is commonly understood as recognition of a child's personhood and her or his ability to take part in decisions that affect her or his life, whether in the family or in the community or the country as a whole. Recognising that people interpreted and understood the term differently, child participation has been described as an 'amoeba term' that is being used in relation to a wide range of situations, including children singing at adult conferences, children answering questions of adult researchers, children educating other children, and also children forming their own organisations. Because the concept draws upon different sources and has taken different routes, there is no unanimity in understanding. It is increasingly being used in the context of political participation (to distinguish itself from participation in the broader and blurred sense), and a number of other terms such as citizenship and protaganism, are being used to overcome over-use or misuse of the term child participation (Theis 2001). More recently the term 'self-determination' has come to be used in the context of children's participation (Ratna: chapter 7).

The right to participation for children gained formal recognition and began to be discussed seriously only after the coming into force of the CRC (Article 12). The UNCRC does not mention the term 'child participation' explicitly but the tone and tenor of its articles advocate a proactive role for children in matters concerning them, upholding an independent personality of the child. Article 12—one of the general principles of the CRC—articulates the real essence of the idea of children's participation. It states the right of children and young people to express their views freely in matters affecting them and that their views should be given due weight in accordance with their age and maturity, for which they should be provided the opportunity to be heard in any judicial and administrative proceeding affecting the child, either directly, or through representatives or an appropriate body in a manner consistent with the procedural rules of national law. This article, in addition to Articles 13, 14 and 15 establishes the child's right to access to information, freedom of belief, and freedom of association, and supports a child's right to participation in family, community, culture and broader civil society.

However, expanding on this Article the General Comment 5 by the UN Committee on the Rights of the Child it states that,[6]

> If consultation is to be meaningful, documents as well as processes need to be made accessible. But appearing to 'listen' to children is relatively unchallenging; giving due weight to their views requires real change. Listening to children should not be seen as an end in itself, but rather as a means by which States make their interactions with children and their actions on behalf of children ever more sensitive to the implementation of children's rights. (Para 12, Article 12)

Although considerable progress has been made in the implementation of Article 12 of the CRC which gives the right to every child capable of forming his or her own views the right to express those views freely in all matters affecting the child, with due weight in accordance with age and maturity, there continues to be the presence of long-standing practices and attitudes, as well as political and economic barriers. Recognising this, the Committee notes,

> While difficulties are experienced by many children, the Committee particularly recognizes that certain groups of children, including younger boys and girls, as well as children belonging to marginalized and

disadvantaged groups, face particular barriers in the
realization of this right. The Committee also remains
concerned about the quality of many of the practices
that do exist. There is a need for a better
understanding of what Article 12 entails and how to
fully implement it for every child. (Para 4)

Therefore, expanding on Article 12, in its General Comment
No.12 on The Right of the Child to be Heard, the Committee
decided to make a distinction between the right to be heard
of an individual child and the right to be heard as applied
to a group of children (e.g., a class of schoolchildren, the
children in a neighbourhood, the children of a country,
children with disabilities, or girls). Explaining this it said,

This is a relevant distinction because the Convention
stipulates that States parties must assure the right
of the child to be heard according to the age and
maturity of the child . . . the views expressed by
children may add relevant perspectives and
experience and should be considered in decision-
making, policymaking and preparation of laws and/
or measures as well as their evaluation. (Para 9)

What is even more important is the emphasis that the
General Comment lays on the fact that including children
should not only be a momentary act, but the starting point
for an intense exchange between children and adults on
the development of policies, programmes and measures in
all relevant contexts of children's lives.

It has been, however, argued that the approach of the
Committee on the Rights of the Child to children's
participation rights under the CRC, has failed to construe
and apply Article 12 in such a way as to address effectively
children's exclusion from democracy and that this gap in
the Committee's jurisprudence necessarily filters down into
the practice of states (Nolan 2010).

What is clear is that participation of children in decisions that matter and concern them will be as per their age and maturity, that is, in a manner consistent with the evolving capacities of the child, and with appropriate guidance in the exercise of the rights by the child (Article 5 of the CRC). This requires that guidance must be provided by adults based on the recognition of the evolving capacity and maturity of the child, making the role of adults in the family, society, community or in government crucial for ensuring the right of the child to participate and be heard. It also necessitates a better understanding of how to provide protection in environments that respect and advance children's capacities (Lansdown 2009).

In the last decade or so, a growing number of non-governmental organisations committed to the realisation of children's rights have been advocating for children's participation. Drawing by and large from their own perspective and experiences and those of other organisations and increasingly from the framework provided by the UNCRC, they have been developing ways and means of enabling, strengthening and promoting children's roles as social actors and their representation in development and discourse (Singh et al. 2006). Children are being involved in research, assessments, monitoring and consultations. They work as peer educators, health promoters and young journalists, mobilisers and leaders of groups and even unions. In many countries, children's clubs, parliaments and youth councils have been formed and in some cases children have been able to influence public decisions and resource allocations (Theis undated). Child-led groups and organisations have been facilitated and even set up non-governmental organisations, support organisations or funders.

Recognising the role of civil society in promoting child participation, the UN Committee on the Rights of the Child states in General Comment 5:

One-off or regular events like Children's Parliaments can be stimulating and raise general awareness. But article 12 requires consistent and ongoing arrangements. Involvement of and consultation with children must also avoid being tokenistic and aim to ascertain representative views. The emphasis on 'matters that affect them' in article 12 (1) implies the ascertainment of the views of particular groups of children on particular issues—for example children who have experience of the juvenile justice system on proposals for law reform in that area, or adopted children and children in adoptive families on adoption law and policy. It is important that Governments develop a direct relationship with children, not simply one mediated through non-governmental organizations (NGOs) or human rights institutions. In the early years of the Convention, NGOs had played a notable role in pioneering participatory approaches with children, but it is in the interests of both Governments and children to have appropriate direct contact. (Para 12)

Duncan has noted that allowing children to make their views known in matters that affect them is yet to gain full acceptance. 'Expressions of the right to participation are rare within child-specific provisions across countries', she says (Duncan 2008: 51 and 52). This is significant, despite notable exceptions such as Article 40 of the Ecuadorean Constitution, Articles 78 and 79 of the Venezuelan Constitution and Article 41(6)(k) of the draft Kenyan Harmonised Constitution.[7] Nolan finds that despite the role of children as political actors during apartheid, the South African Constitution does not make provision for children's participation rights other than providing for a right to legal representation in criminal and, in limited circumstances, civil proceedings and that this contrasts with the significant rise in recognition of the 'protection' and 'provision' rights set out in the UN Convention on the Rights of the Child at the domestic constitutional level (Nolan 2010).[8]

Riggio has found that countries such as the Philippines, Spain, Brazil, the Occupied Palestinian Territory, Colombia, Honduras, Nigeria and Croatia have focused on the opportunity that the Convention on the Rights of the Child offers to develop local systems of governance that include children as a primary concern and even as players. Such experiences have prioritised the development of permanent municipal systems, such as work plans and city-level strategies for children, and partnerships among stakeholders such as the municipal government, mayor, communities, NGOs and children. The Youth Parliament of Albania was a project aimed at increasing youth participation in public debates. Implemented in cooperation with the Albanian Youth Council, the project has established representative assemblies. In Ukraine, the Young People's Health and Development programme strives to promote healthy lifestyles among young people and to develop innovative approaches to fulfilling young people's health and development rights. It is based on a youth participation strategy and has promoted a children's parliamentarian movement in 15 cities and a children's information radio agency in five cities (Riggio 2002).

She further notes that in the context of building a child-inclusive governance system, the municipalities in some countries have focused on making the budget development process more participatory and more transparent. For instance, following the Brazilian model, a participatory budgeting process was developed in Ecuador wherein 18 municipalities were implementing an initiative named Participatory Management and Budget Allocation for Equity with the goal of achieving access to basic social services for all children. Civil society was directly involved in making decisions on municipal resource allocation and citizens contributed to determining the municipal budget, setting priorities and monitoring expenditure. The overall aim was to strengthen governance, support the decentralisation process and ensure a more equitable distribution of resources and involved the Ecuadorian Municipalities Association, NGOs, universities and UN agencies such as UNICEF, UNDP and UNIFEM (ibid.).

What is more, some of these initiatives had shown some encouraging results. In Brazil, participatory budgeting initiated in 1989 in Porto Alegre, the capital of the state of Rio Grande do Sul, had resulted in a direct impact on the quality of life for children. Over a decade, Porto Alegre had reduced its infant mortality rate from 20 to 12 deaths per 1,000 live births. Similar strategies had been adopted by about 200 Brazilian cities, many achieving remarkable improvements in access to basic social services (ibid.).

Although the theory and practice of child participation has evolved considerably in this period, the notion has not been able to make a significant dent in the collective mindset of the social and political institutions and the individuals who comprise them. This is largely because of a lack of conceptual understanding and the appreciation of the value and practicability of child participation. Advocacy for children and with children on a wider scale suffers because there are few experiences to guide us and their value and applicability is defined to a great extent by their context and the issues, lifestyles and characteristics of the children themselves (Singh et al. 2006). Despite this interest in children's participation, most children still do not participate in important decisions affecting them. Schools and education are not participatory and parents do not listen to children. Government decisions are made without children's inputs and the media continue to broadcast images of children as helpless victims or of adolescents as trouble makers (Theis undated).

What is of even greater concern is that there is even a backlash against children's participation. This new resistance is often based on first-hand experiences. Examples include children who burst out crying at press conferences and who complain about being misled by the sponsoring agency of a consultation (ibid.). There are complaints of the same children being used as 'show pieces' again and again at different events; or performers of adult directions; being aggressive or petulant when not given centre stage or first chance to be on stage, even as accompanying adults compete with each other for 'their child representative' to be given the first chance. HAQ's own experience has shown that children are pushed by accompanying adults to be in the fore-front and take front-stage, as the adults see it as their failure if 'their' children are not the 'stars'. Children have walked off the stage, as they were not allowed to be the first one to speak or perform.

In the Philippines, some politicians have lobbied to abolish the nation-wide children's community councils because they are seen to have been manipulated by local elites for their own political agendas. Donor funding was withdrawn from a children's television programme because the children were not seen to sufficiently assist the sponsoring agency to advance its child rights agenda. In Mongolia, efforts to pass a national policy on children's and young people's participation are running into resistance in parliament. These examples show that children's participation may in fact face more obstacles (ibid.).

Needless to say, common to all definitions and interpretations is the understanding that children have a right to be heard in matters that concern them. They must have the opportunity to voice their views and concerns. Children's participation for HAQ remains a value, process and a means rather than a project-driven activity or an end in itself. Therefore, although none of HAQ's programmes are directly focused on addressing child participation, it is recognised as the basic premise and an integral theme of its work. HAQ's legal aid programme ensures that children have a right to be heard in judicial proceedings. Its counselling service ensures that children are 'heard' and their concerns are taken forward wherever necessary, especially making sure that they are heard by their families, parents or guardians. Participation must begin in the family, in the community, in the schools, indeed in their daily lives. Children's rights to participate should not have to wait for an agency to come and facilitate the creation of a children's club or group, or children being taken to events where they can share a platform with adults. Otherwise, Meenal's story that this chapter began with will get repeated again and again.

There is a danger that 'governance *for* children' may be equated with 'governance *with* children'. This may encourage a new kind of marginalisation: the notion that just giving young people a chance to be heard is enough. It is clearly *not* enough. There is a difference between hearing children speak and actually listening to what they have to say. There is additionally a vast difference between listening and responding. It is an oversimplification to suggest that merely giving young people a voice will lead to age-sensitive policies and practices in the absence of follow-through and attention to many other more mundane factors such as regulatory frameworks, impact assessments, budgets, training and monitoring (Bartlett 2005).

Ultimately, the weaknesses in the concept of participation are resulting in a failure to provide a strong enough basis to forge an agenda for children's participation. As Theis points out,

> Participation simply means 'taking part'—but in what? As a concept, participation is an empty vessel that can be filled with almost anything. The popularity of participation among development agencies, donors and even the World Bank, is an indication that participation is a widely acceptable concept. It always stands for something else: volunteering, being involved in decisions, control, power, democracy, freedom, civil rights, demanding entitlements, and holding those in power to account. Participation is also regarded as safe because it has

been stripped of power and politics. As far as children's participation is concerned, the concept does not seem to be able to stand on its own. In order to hold up conceptually, children's participation needs a scaffolding of ladders, degrees, levels, enabling environments and supporting adjectives, such as meaningful and ethical. Part of the failure of children's participation to become a broader movement is its lack of ambition. (Theis undated)

◊

Child Participation in India in Practice

There are several models through which child participation initiatives are undertaken in the country.[9] Some even precede the convention. However, it is with the UNCRC that many more organisations have made it part of their own programming and mandate, many at the behest and with the support of international organisations. In fact there are now forums such as The Forum for Promotion of Child Participation, that Tamil Nadu and Puducherry have initiated. However, at the level of the government child participation still remains a fairly uncharted or unaddressed area.

Different organisations and networks have evolved their own unique models of engaging with children. The ways in which they engage with children depend on specific organisational profile and structure. These approaches sometimes overlap while at times they also complement one another.

The grassroots initiatives usually work directly with children, engaging them and responding to the local issues that impact their lives, which may include children at risk or those belonging to marginalised and/or vulnerable communities, working children, street children, and also children in the villages.

The international NGOs (INGOs) also constantly strive towards changes at the community level, mostly through local groups and organisations. At the same time, they try and influence policy formulation at a global level around issues of children and their rights. INGOs have succeeded in highlighting the issue of children's participation but while they are able to utilise their regional and global experience to introduce new perspectives and ways of engagement, their outreach and the ability to consolidate the micro-level interactions and to connect the micro with macro is dependent on the local partners and their capacities. The networks and alliances, on the other hand, do not emphasise the immediate changes as they seek more lasting changes in the lives of a broader constituency of children.

The resource organisations have multiple objectives as they seek to develop ways and means of working with children as well as contributing to a pool of literature and resources which could be useful for different kinds of agencies and organisations working for child rights.

One of the ways in which most organisations practice children's participation, is by forming children's collectives and organisations with that as the end in mind or for the sake of working with children through the collectives such as clubs, *sanghs,* unions, and do not see these as a means to working with children for realising their rights. They largely follow the process of organising children into groups or clubs such as *bal sabha, bal sangam, bal panchayat,* forum for street and working children, etc. The rationale behind these children's collectives is that such an initiative will help us *recognise children's perspectives.* The recognition of their perspective or the fact that children also have a point of view would help *strengthen children's role as social actors.* Such a process then has the capacity to *strengthen the participatory potential of children* in the larger democratic set up of the country. Once such a form of intervention of including and involving children and listening to their voices becomes an organisational ethos then one could *create an enabling environment for children* (Singh et al. 2006).

Although different organisations or networks have evolved their unique models, some overlapping and complimentary processes can be seen (see Table 1.1).

Table 1.1: Broad trends and patterns of engagement

Organi-sational structure	Relationships, partnerships and likely focus	Strengths	Challenges
NGO	Works directly with speci c groups of children and communities; Greater concern with local issues.	Ability to relate child participa-tion with local context and speci c issues.	Sensitisation of adult commu-nity members in order to work through/with them to seek or represent com-munity-speci c contexts and issues.
Interna-tional NGO	Works mainly in partnerships with local NGOs; Grass-root level interventions are shaped by their reliance on local partners; Likely to focus on promoting children's par-ticipation through orientation, information shar-ing and capacity building.	Innovative practices based on lessons from elsewhere, bring in diverse and varied expertise; Resource base and outreach through the partners allows greater scope for promoting children's par-ticipation.	Need to concen-trate on building capacities and perspectives of local partners; Strive to nur-ture a long-term, sustain-able and organic relationship with the con-stituency of chil-dren that the local networks engage with.
Net-works and cam-paigns	Dependence on partners/mem-bers; Greater con-cern with macro-level issues.	Collective ad-vocacy; Greater impact and visibility, issue driven.	Sustain the spirit and vision of the 'common causes' that need focused advocacy.

Source: Singh et al. (2006).

Through the course of this process documentation of dif-ferent approaches of children's participation emerged. They highlight varying degrees and nature of engagements (ibid.).

Table 1.2 presents the different ways in which organisations and alliances engage with children.

Table 1.2: The nature of engagement

Underlying assumption	Approach	Structure & mechanisms	Factors that seem critical if the assumptions are to be realised
Collectives empower	Organisation of children	Informal	• Platform that allows regular interactions • Facilitation by adults (and by older children) • Inclusion—effort to include children usually marginalised (e.g., younger children, girls, children with disabilities and seemingly less marginalised/relatively well-off children)
		Formal	• Identity of children's organisation that can hold them together • Linkages within and outside the organisation • Inclusion
Children's views are valuable • as informant • as users of knowledge • as researchers	Understanding, recognising & promoting children's perspectives	Creative facilitation of expressions	• Empathy among the adults who are facilitating or are affected by children's views • Facilitation and analytical skills among the adults
		Researches with children	• Empathy • Inclusion • Facilitation, interviewing, analytical and documentation skills
Children can make a difference	Strengthening children's role as social actors	Acknowledgement	• A supportive adult constituency • Universality—acceptance without conditions/caveats
		Opportunity	• Availability of platforms and ideas • Inclusion
		Facilitation	• Facilitation skills and the ability to provide back-up support by adults • Inclusion
Children's abilities, capacities and competences make a difference	Strengthening children's participatory potential	Information	• Easy comprehension by children • Access to and for children • Sharing with and among children
		Skills: analyses, negotiation, representation and leadership	• Creative platforms and learning—adults' ability to innovate • Practical orientation of the interventions and activities • Inclusion

Source: Singh et al. (2006).

However, systematic inclusion of the views of children and their participation is yet to be addressed by the government in any planned way. In its last report to the UN Committee on the Rights of the Child, an attempt was made to involve children in the reporting process with support from UNICEF (Department of Women and Child Development 2001). However, in the section on 'Respect for the Views of the Child (Article 12)', the initiatives that are reported are those by NGOs and civil society groups. Clearly, the government has nothing to report in terms of initiatives taken by it (ibid.).

Since then, child participation has started making inroads into government documents in the country. For example, The National Plan of Action 2005 has a section dedicated to it. The Eleventh Five Year Plan has identified children's participation in policies and programmes as one of the general principles for the review of policies, programmes, services, laws, budgets and procedures for incorporating and integrating better development and protection for children (Government of India 2008: 218). The National Commission for Protection of Child Rights (NCPCR) clearly states, 'The NCPCR believes that child participation is integral to addressing child rights. Therefore the Commission facilitates children's participation to enable children to access their rights and entitlements.... The Commission encourages child participation in each one of its interventions.'[10]

Conclusion

Through their own constitutions and by ratifying international instruments, countries have agreed to ensure implementation of children's rights. Indeed, the promulgation and ratification of the UN Convention on the Rights of the Child brought home the need to recognise the citizenship rights of children to governments as well as organisations working with children. India ratified the CRC in 1992 but there is a need to critically evaluate the adherence to its principles in the country's constitution as well as in the implementation of child-sensitive policies and programmes. Implementation of rights can only be done by formulating legislation, policies and programmes and implementing them through the executive, legislature and judiciary. This is closely linked to the governance system of any country. This in effect means that children as citizens are affected by any action of the government, whether it is directed at them or not. For example, it is unfortunate that the right to a clean and protected earth is clashing with the right to food, as the world's poor are caught up in a struggle between addressing emerging problems arising from climate change and lower levels of food production as recent estimates suggest that increased demand for biofuels accounts for 30 per cent of the recent food crisis (*The Times* 2008). Similarly, agriculture policies that make farmers indigent, even lead to farmer suicides as in India, push children into exploitation and labour to support the families. There is a clear link between children dropping out of school and taking to work due to parental ill-health in the absence of free health care and social security, and increasing costs of health care.

As has been mentioned before, an understanding of good governance with respect to children is essentially about the recognition of children as citizens in their own right, therefore as rights holders. And yet, the most difficult challenge remains the acknowledgement and acceptance of citizenship of children and the relevance of focusing on children in the larger governance and human rights discourse. Across the world, groups, academia and institutions have been working towards developing tools and mechanisms to assess and monitor state performance in realising the rights of children. They are also planning and executing interventions to make governance systems more responsive to children's rights and entitlements. An overview of actions undertaken by them shows that these include analysis of budgets, monitoring the performance of elected representatives in all areas of governance, scanning and critiquing policies, laws and programmes, and interfacing with the government and international bodies. However, there is yet to be a consensus on what constitutes good governance with respect to children and what are the indicators and markers. This is the big task ahead.

The Indian prime minister, Mr Manmohan Singh, at a conference of Congress chief ministers in 2005 said, 'If we look around, what is the happiness index of the average citizen vis-à-vis the government, my own surmise is that there is considerable dissatisfaction with governance and the agents of governance.'[11] Can the situation of children and their well-being be used as an indicator of good governance?

❧

Notes

[1] The child labour law in India prohibits labour in hazardous employment up to 14 years of age.

[2] According to UNSCAP, 'Good governance has 8 major characteristics. It is participatory, consensus oriented, accountable, transparent, responsive, effective and efficient, equitable and inclusive and follows the rule of law. It assures that corruption is minimized, the views of minorities are taken into account and that the voices of the most vulnerable in society are heard in decision-making. It is also responsive to the present and future needs of society.'

[3] These are the three key duties elaborated by the UN Committee on Economic, Social and Cultural Rights based on the Maastricht Guidelines on Violations of Economic, Social and Cultural Rights (Part II, para 6, Maastricht, Netherlands January 22–26, 1997).

[4] Committee on the Rights of the Child, Thirty-fourth session, September 19–October 3, 2003, General Comment No. 5 (2003), General measures of implementation of the Convention on the Rights of the Child (Articles 4, 42 and 44, para 6).

[5] Until 2000, the term in use—both nationally and internationally—for such analysis was Child Budget or

Children's Budget. HAQ, however, chose to use the more appropriate term 'Budget for Children'. While the meaning of the earlier description could be taken to suggest the participation of children—which is not the case at all—the term thus chosen attempted to do away with this unintended suggestion.

[6] Committee on the Rights of the Child, Fifty-first Session, May 25–June 12, 2009, General Comment No. 12 (2009). The Right of the Child To Be Heard. CRC/C/GC/12. July 1, 2009.

[7] • Article 44 provides that children and adolescents have, amongst other things, the right to social participation and to be consulted in matters affecting them. It also states that the state guarantees their freedom of expression and association, the free operation of student councils and other forms of association (translation by A. Nolan [2010]).

• Articles 78 and 79 of the Venezuelan constitution provide respectively (amongst other things) that the state must promote children's progressive incorporation into active citizenship, and that young people have the right and duty to be active participants in the development process (cited in Nolan 2010).

• Article 41(6)(k) states that every child has a right 'to know of decisions affecting the child, express an opinion and have that opinion taken into account, taking into consideration the age and maturity of the child and the nature of the decision'(cited in ibid.).

[8] Section 35 of the South African Constitution (cited in Nolan 2010).
Ibid., Section 28(1)(h)(cited in ibid.).

[9] This section is based on Singh et al. (2006).

[10] See ncpcr.gov.in/child_participation, accessed on January 13, 2011.

[11] At the conference of Congress chief ministers, October 8, 2005.

ℒ

References

Abdellatif, Adel M. (Programme Advisor, Regional Bureau for Arab States, UNDP). 2003. *Good Governance and Its*

Relationship to Democracy & Economic Development. Workshop IV, Democracy, Economic Development, and Culture, Global Forum III on Fighting Corruption and Safeguarding Integrity, Seoul, 20–31 May, Ministry of Justice, Republic of Korea and UNESCAP, available at http://www.undppogar.org/publications/governance/aa/goodgov.pdf, accessed on May 1, 2007.

African Child Policy Forum. 2008. *The African Report on Child Well-being: How Friendly Are African Governments?* The African Child Policy Forum, Addis Ababa, Ethiopia.

Bartlett, Sheridan. 2005. 'Good Governance: Making Age Part of the Equation—An Introduction', *Children, Youth and Environments* 15(2): 1–17, available at http://www.colorado. edu/journals/cye, accessed on September 30, 2009.

Bequele, Assefa. 2009. 'Governance and Child Well-being: Lessons from Africa', Proceedings of the International Colloquium on Children and Governance: Holding the State Accountable, organised by HAQ: Centre for Child Rights, July 20–22, New Delhi, India.

Brinkerhoff, Derick. 2003. *Accountability and Health Systems: Overview, Framework, and Strategies*, pp. 5–7. The Partners for Health Reform*plus* Project, Abt Associates Inc., Bethesda, MD.

Casseim, Shaamela, Helen Perry, Masteora Sadan and Judith Streak. 2000. 'Are Poor Children Being Put First? Child Poverty and the Budget', Idasa Budget Information Service (BIS).

Department of Women and Child Development. 2001. Convention on the Rights of the Child, India, First Periodic Report, Ministry of Human Resources Development, Government of India, New Delhi, India.

———. 2004. Convention on the Rights of the Child, India, First Periodic Report 2001 which came up before the Committee on January 21, Ministry of Human Resources Development, Government of India, New Delhi, India.

Duncan, Beatrice. 2008. *Constitutional Reforms in Favor of Children*, UNICEF, 2008, pp. 27, 52, available at http://www.unicef.org/policyanalysis/files/Constitutional_Reforms_in_Favour_of_Children.doc, accessed on September 30, 2009.

Ennew, Judith, Hastadewi Yuli and Dominique Pierre Plateau. 2004. *Seen and Heard: Participation of Children and Young People in Southeast, East Asia and Pacific in Events and Forums Leading to and Following Up on the United Nations General Assembly Special Session for Children, 2002*, Save the Children Southeast, East Asia and Pacific Region, Bangkok.

Ganguly, S. P. 2000. *Central Government Budgets in India: An Analysis*, Concept Publishing House, New Delhi, India.

Government of India. 2008. Eleventh Five Year Plan, Volume II, Planning Commission, New Delhi.

Government of South Africa. 1999. National Programme of Action for Children in South Africa (NPA), President's Office, South Africa.

HAQ: Centre for Child Rights. 2002. *Children in Globalising India: Challenging Our Conscience*, HAQ, New Delhi, India.

———. 2005. *Status of Children in India Inc.*, HAQ, New Delhi, India.

———. 2008. *Still out of Focus—Status of Children in India*, HAQ, New Delhi, India.

———. 2009. Proceedings of the International Colloquium on Children and Governance: Holding the State Accountable, July 20–22, HAQ, New Delhi, India.

India Alliance on Child Rights. 2003. Every Right for Every Child, Citizens' Alternate Review and Report on India's Progress Towards CRC Realisation in Response to First Periodic Report (2001). Submitted to the UN Committee on the Rights of the Child, India Alliance on Child Rights, New Delhi, India.

Inter-Agency Working Group on Children's Participation (IAWGCP). 2008. *Children as Active Citizens—A Policy and Programme Guide. Commitments and Obligations for Children's Civil Rights and Civic Engagement in East Asia and the Pacific*, Inter-Agency Working Group on Children's Participation (IAWGCP), ECPAT International, Knowing Children, Plan International, Save the Children Sweden, Save the Children UK, UNICEF and World Vision, Bangkok, Thailand.

Lansdown, Gerison. 2009. *'Evolving Capacities' Explained in Measuring Maturity: Understanding Children's 'Evolving*

Capacities', CRIN Review, October 23, Child Rights Information Network, London, UK, available at http://www.crin.org/docs/CRIN_review_23_final.pdf, accessed on January 13, 2011.

Planning Commission, Government of India. 2008. *Towards Women's Agency and Child Rights* in the Eleventh Five Year Plan (2007–2012), volume II, Social Sector, pp. 202–19. Oxford University Press, New Delhi, India.

Ministry of Women and Child Development, Government of India. 2005. *National Plan of Action for Children*, New Delhi, India.

Mitlin, Diana. 2004. 'Reshaping Local Democracy', *Environment and Urbanisation*, 16(1): 3–8. Cited in Sheridan Bartlett, 2005, 'Good Governance: Making Age a Part of the Equation— An Introduction', *Children Youth and Environments* 15(2): 1–17. Available at http://www.colorado.edu/journals/cye, p. 1, accessed on September 30, 2009.

Nolan, Aoife. 2010. 'The Child as "Democratic Citizen"— Challenging the "Participation Gap" ', *Public Law*, October: 126–41. Available at SSRN: http://ssrn.com/abstract= 1680810, accessed on March 17, 2010.

Oudenhoven, Nico van and Rekha Wazir. 2006. *Newly Emerging Needs of Children, An Exploration*, Garant, Antwerp, pp. 23, 26 and 31.

Potts, Helen. Undated. *Accountability and Right to the Highest Attainable Standard of Health*, Human Rights Centre, UK and Open Society Institute, Public Health Program, USA.

Riggio, Eliana. 2002. 'Child Friendly Cities: Good Governance in the Best Interest of the Child', *Environment and Urbanisation*, 14(2): 45–58.

Save the Children. 2003 and 2004. *Children and Young People as Citizens. Partners for Social Change. Overview. Promoting Children and Young People Participation and Citizenship Rights in South and Central Asia*, International Save the Children Alliance, Kathmandu, Nepal.

Sheahan, Frances. 2009. Getting Away With It: The Role of International Mechanisms in Holding States Accountable. Proceedings of the International Colloquium on Children and Governance: Holding the State Accountable, organised by HAQ: Centre for Child Rights, July 20–22, New Delhi, India.

Singh, Neelam and Ravi Karkara. 2002. Child Participation. Children in Globalising India: Challenging our Conscience, HAQ: Centre for Child Rights, New Delhi, India.

Singh, Neelam, Ruchika Negi and Subhashim Goswami. 2006. Experiences in Engaging with Children in Developmental Processes: Process Documentation of Some Organisations and Networks, Mimeo, HAQ: Centre for Child Rights and UNICEF, New Delhi, India.

The Times. 2008. 'Cut Bio Fuel Targets to Feed the Poor, Leaders are Urged', June 3, by Richard Owen in Rome and Jill Sherman, Whitehall Editor, available at http://www.timesonline.co.uk/tol/news/world/europe/article4053744.ece, accessed on January 13, 2011.

Theis, Jochim. Undated. *Children as Active Citizens—An Agenda for Children's Civil Rights and Civil Engagement in East Asia and the Pacific*, Unpublished, Bangkok, Thailand.

———. 2001. *Children's Rights and Participation—Some Points for Discussion* (unpublished), Save the Children, Bangkok, Thailand. Cited in Neelam Singh and Ravi Karkara, 2002, *Child Participation*, Children in Globalising India: Challenging our Conscience, HAQ: Centre for Child Rights, New Delhi, India.

UN Committee on the Rights of the Child. 2000. 23rd Session, Consideration of Reports Submitted by States Parties Under Article 44 of the Convention, Concluding Observations of the Committee on the Rights of the Child: India CRC/C/15/Add. 115, January 28.

———. 2004. 23rd Session, Consideration of Reports Submitted by States Parties Under Article 44 of the Convention, Concluding Observations of the Committee on the Rights of the Child: India CRC/C/15/Add. 228, February 26.

UNESCAP. 2009. *What is Good Governance?* Available at http://www. unescap.org/pdd/prs/ProjectActivities/Ongoing/gg/governance.asp, accessed on October 15, 2009.

Van Bueren, Geraldine. 1995. The International Law on the Rights of the Child, Martinus Nijhoff Publishers, The Hague, Netherlands, p. 13.

2

Governance and Child Well-being: Evidence and Lessons from Africa

Assefa Bequele

Introduction

Africa is a very young continent, the youngest in the world.[1] Children under 18 constitute some 51.5 per cent of the population, with the ratio being as high as 54.8 per cent in Nigeria, 55.2 per cent in Ethiopia, and 60.8 per cent in Uganda. That it is so can be a blessing but also a potential curse. The extent to which African governments respect children and protect them from harm and abuse, and provide them with opportunities for a healthy and productive life has an impact both on the future of the children concerned and the future of the region. A healthy, well-fed and educated child population is a necessary foundation for a modern, productive and knowledge-based economy that can effectively participate in today's globalised world.

Similarly, the way our society raises and treats our children at home and in school is critical for what they will be as adults and citizens. A child growing up in an environment where he sees his mother beaten by the father, where girls are discriminated and excluded, where differing views and opinions are not tolerated, and where choices are not negotiated is unlikely to be the builder of a peaceful and democratic order.

Here are some facts about the children of Africa:

- Over a third of children less than five years old suffered from moderate to severe stunting in 2006;

- Each year some one million babies are stillborn; about half a million die on their first day; and, at least one million babies die in their first month of life;
- As if this is not enough, we now face a huge and growing orphan population, estimated at, for example, 20 per cent of the under-15 population in Congo (Brazzaville), Rwanda, Uganda, Malawi, Zambia and Zimbabwe. Look at the absolute number of orphans in selected countries: 4.2 million in DR Congo, 4.8 million in Ethiopia and a staggering 8.6 million in Nigeria. According to the African Child Policy Forum (ACPF), the orphan population in sub-Saharan Africa could, within a couple of years' time, be equal to the size of the combined populations of South Africa, Botswana, Swaziland and Lesotho;
- There is then the problem of violence against children. This is a widespread problem throughout Africa and is found at home, at schools, at work and in the community. In an ACPF survey of violence against girls in Uganda, Ethiopia and Kenya, over 90 per cent of the girls surveyed reported being victims of one form of violence or another. Female Genital Mutilation (FGM) is deeply ingrained and early marriage a common practice;
- Finally, access to schooling. Briefly, despite the progress, fewer than half of the children of primary school age in Sub-Saharan Africa go to school. These are some of the facts. In far too many countries, children are given an inferior place in the scheme of things, at home or in the larger community.

So, what then is being done and, perhaps more pointedly, how much effort is being exerted by African governments to address these challenges?

In policy analysis as in life, the obvious can sometimes be the least visible and discernible. It now comes as a surprise to many of us, though it should have been manifestly clear long ago that, after all is said and done, governance is the key for the realisation of child rights and well-being. What governments do in the form of policies and effective implementation is fundamental to effect sustained and lasting change in the conditions of children.

Our governments, like most others in Asia and Latin America, have an impressive record in their formal accession to the relevant international treaties on children. However, the extent of their commitment varies widely, and the gap between promises and reality remains wide in many countries. Why? Which governments are doing well and which ones are not? How do governments—in this case African—rank in relation to each other? What accounts for differences in government performance? To what extent are such differences due to disparities in levels of development or levels of poverty? ACPF is a pan-African policy research and advocacy centre. As such, much of its work focuses on public policy and government performance and these were some of the questions that we tried to address in a recent report, *The African Report on Child Wellbeing 2008: How Child-friendly are African Governments?* and this essay is based on this report. In order to address these questions, we needed to develop a normative and statistical framework that facilitates comparison among governments and simplifies understanding and analysis. Such a framework should ideally provide the opportunity to spell out clearly and easily (a) the specific commitments made and actions taken, (b) the statistical and quantitative data and evidence needed to assess actions, outcomes and progress, (c) the mechanism for scoring and ranking achievement, and (d) the specific areas where a country is doing well and those where it should exert more effort. What in other words accounts for differences in government performance and what are the policy lessons and conclusions?

This report uses the concept of child-friendliness and a child-friendliness index to assess, score and rank the performance of 52 African governments (those not covered being Somalia and Saharawi Arab Republic). The ACPF developed a methodology with which to measure governments' performance in realising child rights and ensuring their well-being. This measurement approach seeks to assess the extent to which African governments meet their international, regional and constitutional obligations to children, and thus provides an indication of how prioritised children's issues are in governments' policy agendas, and the extent to which those agendas are child-friendly. Performance evaluation involves qualitative and quantitative methods of assessment.

It was while doing this report that we concluded that child deprivation and child well-being are very much matters of governance.

Conceptualising Child Well-being

The well-being in developing countries (WeD) conceptual framework broadly defines well-being as arising from the 'resources retained, acquired and lost', 'needs met or denied', and peoples' experiences and evaluations of these processes, that is, the quality of life ahead (Newton 2007:16). This concept highlights the interplay between the material, cognitive and relational dimensions of well-being, as well its subjective and objective dimensions. Focusing on the discussion on well-being as it refers to children, we come across two apparently contrasting concepts: child well-being as it refers to the present well-being of children and child well-becoming (Ben-Arieh 2006), which is used to describe a future-oriented focus (i.e., preparing children for a productive and happy adulthood). Both perspectives, that of children as persons of today and children in their future status, are legitimate and necessary, both for social science and for public policy. Marrying both these perspectives allows us to arrive at a child-centred perspective where the focus is on child well-being as active members of society now, as well as on the implications of their current well-being for their lives and roles in the future. This child rights-based perspective of child well-being, also called the 'whole child rights perspective', defines child well-being 'as the realisation of child rights and the fulfilment of the opportunity for every child to be all she or he can be in the light of a child's abilities, potential and skills, and as a result of the effective protection and assistance provided by families, communities and the State' (UNICEF 2006).

Child well-being means a lot of things. It is about children being safe, well, healthy and happy. It is about children's opportunities to grow and to learn. It is about positive personal and social relationships, and about being and feeling secure and respected. It is also about being given a voice and being heard. In short, it is about the full and harmonious development of each child's personality, skills and talents. All of these have a better chance of being achieved in societies and states that uphold, both in law and in practice, the principle of the 'best interests of the child'. This means respecting, protecting and realising the rights of children and nurturing a social ecology that provides opportunities for all children—boys and girls, disabled or disadvantaged—to become all that their abilities and their potential allow them to be.

Families are the first of the many actors providing first-line protection to the child and ensuring his or her well-being. As the primary guardians of child well-being, the views, perceptions and practices of families determine the way children are treated and cared for, but two things need to be noted. First, however much they are the source of love and care, families can also, for one reason or another, be the source of child abuse, violence and exploitation. Second, however enlightened and sensitive families may be towards the best interests of their children, their effectiveness will depend on their ability and capacity to provide for their children's physical, intellectual and material needs. It thus becomes important to ensure the survival of the family, and to strengthen its capacity to nurture and raise children.

African communities and traditions also play a central role in ensuring children's well-being. Africa owes its resilience in the face of various forms of distress—including poverty, disease, hostile physical and climatic conditions and the HIV/AIDS pandemic—to these actors.

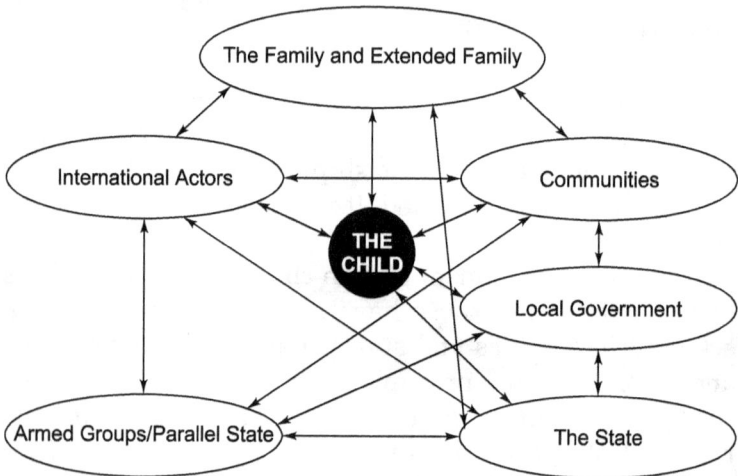

Fig. 2.1: *Conceptual framework of child well-being in Africa*

Source: ACPF (2008: 121).

Child Well-being and Governance

The state is the other indispensable actor in child well-being, and the principal duty bearer of child rights. Thus the state's obligations to respect children's rights, to provide them with full protection, and to fulfill their needs lies at the heart of the rights-based approach to child well-being stipulated in the major child rights instruments—international and national. This is linked to governance in any country.

Good governance is now taking centre stage in the development discussion, for leaders, citizens and children alike. In a survey conducted by ACPF and UNICEF in eight African countries, children ranked good governance as the first characteristic making a country a better place to live in, followed by decreased poverty and a better economic situation. Good governance is, in the words of former President Thambo Mbeki of South Africa, 'critically important . . . to end political and economic mismanagement on our continent, and the consequential violent conflicts, instability, denial of democracy and human rights, deepening poverty and global marginalisation' (ACPF 2008: 2).

The UN Convention on the Rights of the Child (article 27) obliges states to recognise the right of every child to a standard of living adequate for the child's physical, mental, spiritual, moral and social development; or, in the words of the African Charter (article 5[2]), to ensure to the maximum extent possible the survival, protection and development of the child. These two instruments go further, re-drawing the relationship between the state and families as well as between the state and traditions, by entrusting an enhanced role to the state in ensuring the rights and well-being of children. These legal instruments challenged the customarily 'unquestionable' control parents exerted over their children, and outlawed some traditional practices within families that were doing harm to children.

Child-friendliness is a manifestation of the political will of governments to make the maximum effort to meet their obligations to respect, protect and fulfil children's rights and ensure their well-being.

Conceptualising the Child-friendliness of Governments

The child-friendliness index developed by ACPF quantitatively assesses the extent to which African governments are committed to child well-being. In other words, the measurement provides an indication of how important children are in governments' policy agenda, and highlights the extent to which they are child-friendly. The performance scores that result from the exercise serve as measures of a government's effort in ensuring child well-being relative to others. Governments with low performance scores should take it as a signal that they need to improve the implementation of child rights and ensure child well-being. On the other hand, governments with relatively high scores must not use them as an excuse for complacency because it should be realised that the overall state of children's well-being in the continent is far from satisfactory, and there is always room for improvement.

Definition of a child-friendly government
Child friendliness is a manifestation of the political will of governments to put in place pro-child policies and commit resources to realising child rights and ensuring their overall well-being.
  We therefore define a child-friendly government as:

> 'one that is making the maximum effort to meet its obligation to respect, protect and fulfil child rights, and ensure child well-being'.

Source: ACPF (2008: 6).

Three dimensions of child-friendliness emanating from the principles underpinning the Convention on the Rights of the Child and the African Charter on the Rights and Welfare of the Child (ACRWC), were identified, namely the extent to which a government is committed to the principles of:

  (i) **Protection** of children through appropriate legal and policy frameworks
 (ii) **Provision** for the basic needs of children, assessed in terms of budgetary allocation and well-being outcomes
(iii) **Participation** of children in decisions that affect their well-being.

Though child participation is important, it was not possible to obtain sufficient data, and therefore this dimension was not included in the development of the child-friendliness index. The index, thus, covers only the protection and provision components of child well-being.

The dimension on child protection measures governments' overall efforts to protect children against harm, abuse and exploitation through the effective provision of appropriate laws and policies. The following key components have been identified and assessed to determine governments' performances in putting in place relevant laws and policies for the protection of children:

(i) Ratification of international and regional legal instruments relating to children

(ii) Provisions in national laws to protect children against harm and exploitation

(iii) Existence of a juvenile justice system, National Plan of Action (NPA) and coordinating bodies for the implementation of children's rights

(iv) Policy for free primary education.

Provision is measured using two sub-dimensions: budgetary commitment and child-related outcomes. The sub-dimension on budgetary commitment measures governments' efforts in terms of the financial inputs they have channelled to sectors most likely to benefit children. It sheds light on the extent to which governments are committing available budgetary resources to the cause of children. The other sub-dimension on child-related outcomes, on the other hand, measures governments' efforts in light of the outcomes reflected on children themselves. These two sub-dimensions of provision are deliberately categorised as 'input' and 'outcome' measures to analyse and examine separately the efforts that are made along these lines. In addition to the valuable information generated by analysing them separately, the combined measure also shows the overall effort exerted to provide for the basic needs of children and ensure their well-being.

Among the indicators used to measure governments' budgetary commitment are:

   (i) Government expenditure on health as a percentage of total government expenditure;

  (ii) Total public expenditure on education as a percentage of GDP;

 (iii) Percentage of the budget for routine Expanded Programme on Immunisation (EPI) vaccines financed by the government;

 (iv) Military expenditure as a percentage of GDP; and

  (v) Percentage change in governments' expenditure on health since the year 2000.

A rights-based approach is used to measure child-friendliness of governments in terms of their effort to fulfil rights. Child rights include civic, political, social, economic and cultural rights. These rights are interdependent and interrelated, universal and indivisible; and these complex interrelationships between rights and responsibilities require a multidimensional approach to measurement (Bradshaw et al. 2006). Accordingly, the measurement of a government's child-friendliness index follows a multidimensional approach. The phenomenon being measured here is the effort of governments in terms of inputs that they have channelled for realising the rights of children, and outcomes they have succeeded in providing for the needs of children.

The index uses a common framework for the organisation and analysis of information and data for all the 52 countries. It is based on some 40 policy and well-being indicators (see Figure 2.2) and assesses the individual and relative performance of all 52 governments at a point in time (2004–5) and over time (between 1999–2001 and 2004–5).

INDICATORS

Legal and Policy Framework
- UN Convention on the Rights of the Child
- African Charter on the Rights and Welfare of the Child
- Optional Protocol to the Convention on the Rights of the Child on the Sale of Children, Child Prostitution and Pornography
- Optional Protocol to the Convention on the Rights of the Child on the Involvement of Children in Armed Conflict
- ILO Convention on Minimum Age for Admission to Employment (ILO Convention No. 138)
- ILO Convention on the Worst Forms of Child Labour Convention (ILO Convention No. 182)
- International Convention on the Rights of Persons with Disabilities
- The Hague Convention on Intercountry Adoption
- Minimum age for admission to employment
- Minimum age for criminal responsibility
- Minimum age for marriage (both for male and female)
- Existence of juvenile justice systems/child friendly courts
- Existence of a national plan of action for survival, protection and development of children
- Existence of a government body that coordinates and monitors the national strategy for children
- Policy for free education
- Existence of domestic laws on:
  Child trafficking
  Sexual exploitation of children and pornography
  Prohibition of corporal punishment
  Harmful traditional practices

Resource Commitment
- Government expenditure on health as percentage of total government expenditure*
- Percentage of the budget for routine Expanded Programme on Immunisation (EPI) financed by government
- Total public expenditure on education as percentage of GDP
- Military expenditure as percentage of GDP

Child-Related Services/Outcomes
- Percentage of pregnant women attending antenatal care
- Percentage of deliveries attended by skilled health workers
- Percentage of children aged 12-23 months immunised against measles*
- Percentage of children aged 12-23 months immunised against measles*
- Proportion of children with an acute respiratory tract infection or suspected pneumonia who were taken to a health facility
- Number of physicians per hundred thousand population
- Percentage of children underweight
- Infant mortality rate*
- Percentage of population using improved drinking water source*
- Percentage of population using adequate sanitation facilities*
- Gross enrolment rate for primary education by gender
- Gross enrolment rate for secondary education by gender
- Gender difference in enrolment
- Pupil-teacher ratio (Primary)

COMPONENTS/SUB-DIMENSIONS
- Ratification of international and regional legal instruments relating to children***
- National laws/policies/mechanisms***
- National budget expenditure
- Access to health services***
- Access to education***

DIMENSIONS

PROTECTION DIMENSION (Legal and Policy Framework)

BUDGETARY COMMITMENT SUB-DIMENSION

CHILD-RELATED OUTCOMES SUB-DIMENSION

PROVISION DIMENSION

CHILD-FRIENDLINESS INDEX

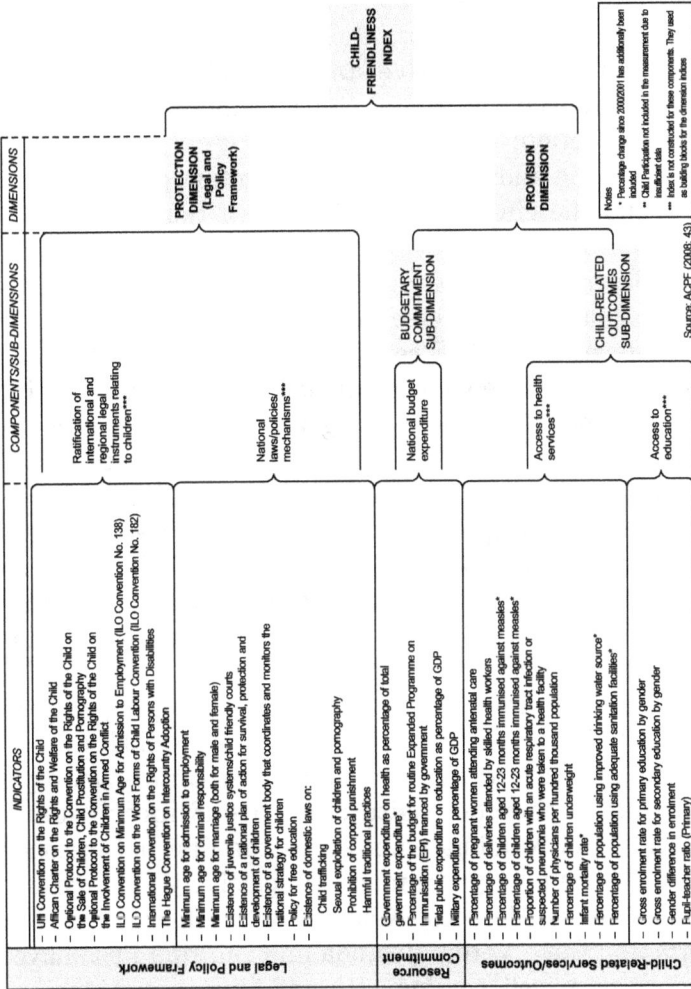

Notes:
* Percentage change since 2000/2001 has additionally been included
** Child Participation not included in the measurement due to insufficient data
*** Index is not constructed for these components. They used as building blocks for the dimension indices

Source: ACPF (2008: 43)

Fig. 2.2: *Child-Friendliness Index (CFI): Indicators, components and dimensions*

Source: ACPF (2008: 43).

Most and Least Child-friendly Governments

In order to evaluate the performance of governments, ACPF followed a three-step approach:

- (i) Scoring and ranking them in terms of protection, that is, their relative standing in laying down the appropriate legal and policy frameworks for child protection;

- (ii) Scoring and ranking their budgetary commitment and the effectiveness with which they used their resources; and

- (iii) Scoring and ranking their overall performance in terms of *both* protection and provision.

Therefore, the ACPF report looked at all 52 African countries and scored and ranked their performance in respect of protection policies, budgetary allocation and child well-being outcomes, and finally their performance in all these areas. This approach helped us to examine performance in various policy domains and identify the policy areas where a particular government is doing well or where it should exert greater effort. Thus, a country may be doing well in the provision of legal protection but not so well in the budgetary area, or vice versa.

As can be seen from Table 2.1, countries are grouped into five areas: *Most Child-friendly, Child-friendly; Fairly Child-friendly, Less Child-friendly* and *Least Child-friendly*. According to the composite child-friendliness index, Mauritius and Namibia emerged as the first and second most child-friendly governments respectively followed by Tunisia, Libya, Morocco, Kenya, South Africa, Malawi, Algeria and Cape Verde. Rwanda and Burkina Faso have also done very well, coming 11th and 12th respectively in the child-friendliness index ranking despite their low economic status.

Table 2.1: Child-Friendliness Index (CFI) values and
ranking of African governments

Country	Index value	Rank	Category
Mauritius	0.711	1	Most child-friendly
Namibia	0.705	2	
Tunisia	0.701	3	
Libya	0.694	4	
Morocco	0.693	5	
Kenya	0.680	6	
South Africa	0.672	7	
Malawi	0.663	8	
Algeria	0.654	9	
Cape Verde	0.651	10	
Rwanda	0.649	11	Child-friendly
Burkina Faso	0.648	12	
Madagascar	0.637	13	
Botswana	0.635	14	
Senegal	0.634	15	
Seychelles	0.634	16	
Egypt	0.632	17	
Mali	0.629	18	
Lesotho	0.624	19	
Burundi	0.622	20	
Uganda	0.611	21	Fairly child-friendly
Nigeria	0.609	22	
United Republic of Tanzania	0.602	23	
Gabon	0.579	24	
Mozambique	0.571	25	
Togo	0.569	26	
Zambia	0.567	27	
Mauritania	0.564	28	
Ghana	0.557	29	
Djibouti	0.552	30	
Dem. Rep. Congo	0.551	31	
Niger	0.545	32	

Country	Index value	Rank	Category
Cameroon	0.537	33	
Congo	0.534	34	
Angola	0.530	35	
Côte d'Ivoire	0.525	36	
Zimbabwe	0.518	37	**Less**
Equatorial			**child-friendly**
Guinea	0.518	38	
Sudan	0.508	39	
Sierra Leone	0.507	40	
Benin	0.506	41	
Ethiopia	0.503	42	
Comoros	0.501	43	
Guinea	0.500	44	
Swaziland	0.494	45	
Chad	0.482	46	
Liberia	0.478	47	**Least**
São Tomé and			**child-friendly**
Principe	0.476	48	
Gambia	0.461	49	
Central African			
Republic	0.445	50	
Eritrea	0.442	51	
Guinea-Bissau	0.366	52	

Source: ACPF (2008: 7).

These and the other countries that emerged in the top 10 or 20 did so mainly for three reasons. First, they put in place appropriate legal provisions to protect children against abuse and exploitation. Second, they allocated a relatively higher share of their budgets to provide for the basic needs of children. Finally, they used resources effectively and were able to achieve favourable well-being outcomes as reflected on children themselves.

At the other extreme are the 10 least child-friendly governments in Africa, these being Guinea-Bissau preceded by Eritrea, Central African Republic, Gambia, São Tomé and Principe, Liberia, Chad, Swaziland, Guinea and Comoros. Of course, the political and economic situation and the underlying causes vary from one country to another. But, by and large, the poor performance or low score of these governments is the result of the actions they failed to take, specifically their failure to institute protective legal and policy instruments, the absence of child-sensitive juvenile justice systems, and the very low budgets allocated to children. For example, government expenditure on health as a percentage of total government expenditure was only 3.5 per cent in Guinea-Bissau, compared with a median average of 9 per cent for the region. Central African Republic also spent only 1.4 per cent of its GDP for education in 2006, compared to the regional average of 4.3 per cent around that time. Eritrea, the country that ranked the second lowest in the child-friendliness index, scored the lowest in budgetary allocation and highest in military spending which stood at 19.3 per cent of GDP in 2004–05.

Economic Status and Child-friendliness

A recurring explanation or excuse given by governments for poor performance is their limited financial capacity, their low level of development and lack of resources. To what extent is this true? In order to answer this question, we compared (a) ranking in budgetary allocations and (b) child-friendliness index rankings with per capita GDP.

Table 2.2 presents countries that have performed both well and poorly in budget allocation in comparison with their economic status. As can be seen, the governments of Malawi, Burkina Faso, Niger, Burundi, DRC and Mali came out as exemplary. The government of Malawi, for instance, ranked first in budgetary commitment, though it has the 45th lowest GDP per capita in Africa. Conversely, Equatorial Guinea ranked 44th in budgetary allocation though it had the highest GDP per capita in Africa in 2005.

Table 2.2: Ranking budgetary commitment
relative to GDP per capita 2004–5

Countries which moved up in ranking for budgetary commitment		Countries which moved down in ranking for budgetary commitment	
Country	Number of places	Country	Number of places
Malawi	+45	Congo (Brazzaville)	−19
Burkina Faso	+34	Guinea	−21
Niger	+26	Libya	−22
Burundi	+23	Angola	−23
Dem. Rep. Congo	+23	Comoros	−24
Mali	+22	Sudan	−26
Togo	+17	Equatorial Guinea	−43

Source: ACPF (2008: 66).

The conclusion is simple, and perhaps not surprising: budgetary commitment is not necessarily related to economic status. There are many poor countries that are committed to children despite economic difficulties. And, there are countries that are doing well economically, but not investing proportionately on their children. Notable among these is Equatorial Guinea, which lies on opposite extremes of the rankings for budgetary commitment and GDP per capita. The governments of Sudan, Comoros, Angola and Libya also performed poorly, moving down 26, 24, 23 and 22 places, respectively, in their rankings for budgetary commitment compared to their position on the economic ladder.

Similarly, our analysis also shows that the child-friendliness index ranking of a country is not necessarily related to its economic status as measured by per capita GDP. A number of governments with relatively low GDP have still managed to score high in 'child-friendliness' (see Table 2.3). Thus the child-friendliness scores for Malawi and Burundi was found to be 38 and 30 places higher respectively than their respective GDP per capita rankings. Such differences were also observed in the rankings of the governments of Madagascar, Rwanda, Burkina Faso, Mali and DRC. For example, the child-friendliness rank of the governments of Madagascar and Rwanda moved 28 and 27 places up, respectively, compared to their GDP per capita ranking.

Table 2.3: Child-Friendliness Index and
GDP per capita ranking 2004–05

Countries which moved up in ranking		Countries which moved down in ranking	
Country	Number of places	Country	Number of places
Malawi	38	Guinea	−16
Burundi	30	Côte d'Ivoire	−17
Madagascar	28	Sudan	−17
Rwanda	27	Gabon	−18
Burkina Faso	25	Angola	−19
Mali	21	Congo	−19
Dem. Rep. Congo	20	Gambia	−19
Kenya	18	Swaziland	−33
Uganda	15	Equatorial Guinea	−37

Source: ACPF (2008: 85).

Conversely, some governments with relatively higher GDP were found to be in the least child-friendly category, as they had failed to put in place appropriate legal and policy frameworks to protect children against exploitation and to use their resources to bring about changes in the well-being of their children. Equatorial Guinea ranks first in terms of GDP per capita, but its ranking in child-friendliness is 37 places lower, indicating that its high economic performance is not benefiting children. The governments of Swaziland, Gambia, Congo (Brazzaville) and Angola could also have done better in utilising their resources for improving the

well-being of children. The analysis showed that 16 countries are 10 or more places lower in their child-friendliness
ranking than their GDP per capita ranking. This indicates
the ample, unutilised potential for improvement in utilisation of resources and for investment in programmes that
target children.

Figure 2.3 summarises the picture by positioning
governments in accordance with their performance in terms
of child-friendliness and GDP per capita. The upper left
quadrant shows the governments that have performed well
and are child-friendly, *despite* their low economic status.
Governments in the upper right quadrant are those with
higher economic performance that also did well in their
degree of child-friendliness. The lower right quadrant shows
the worst scenario. Governments in this particular quadrant
are those with high GDP per capita and poor performance
in relation to the realisation of child well-being. The lower
left quadrant includes governments with low rankings in
both areas.

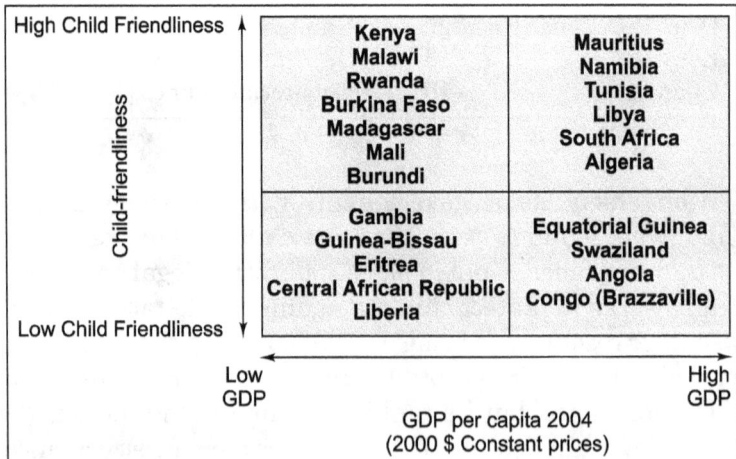

High Child Friendliness	
Kenya Malawi Rwanda Burkina Faso Madagascar Mali Burundi	Mauritius Namibia Tunisia Libya South Africa Algeria
Gambia Guinea-Bissau Eritrea Central African Republic Liberia	Equatorial Guinea Swaziland Angola Congo (Brazzaville)

Child-friendliness

Low Child Friendliness

Low GDP   High GDP

GDP per capita 2004
(2000 $ Constant prices)

Source: ACPF (2008: 86).

Fig. 2.3: *Governments' child-friendliness versus GDP per capita*

Figure 2.3 shows that, despite their relatively low GDPs, Kenya, Malawi, Rwanda and Burkina Faso are among the best performers in Africa; they are among the 12 countries that have made the greatest effort to put in place an adequate legal foundation for the protection of their children and for meeting their basic needs. On the other hand, relatively wealthy countries, with relatively high GDPs— Equatorial Guinea and Angola, for example—are not investing sufficient budgetary resources in children, and so have not scored well in the child-friendliness index ranking, coming out 38th and 35th, respectively.

The child-friendliness index data strongly confirms the fact that governments with a relatively low GDP can still do well in realising child rights and well-being. The missing factor is political will, reflected in misplaced priorities and the clouded vision of governments as to what constitutes the long-term interest of their countries. In other words, it is politics and not economics that is the decisive factor for differences in government performance and child well-being.

Conclusions

Two important conclusions emerge from this exercise. The first has to do with methodology, and hence with the approach taken to analyse comparative performance and the optimal policy mix. It should be pointed out right away that the construction of indices to measure progress is fraught with conceptual, methodological and statistical problems. This is true of indices that deal with social, political and development issues, for example, governance, economic performance and well-being. So also, with the child-friendliness index developed by ACPF.

The concept of friendliness itself is a highly values-loaded term. Friendliness is more than the provision of pro-children laws or budgets. There are other important elements that contribute to the friendliness of a society, state or community. But, how do you measure or quantify the

sociocultural and psychological parameters as well as the
ecological and politically induced environmental factors that
can have a bearing on individual and community well-being
in a sensible and convincing way?

Moreover, there are equity issues. For example, a government's budgetary allocation may give us an idea of how
much a government is concerned with children's issues at
the macro level. But, it does not necessarily indicate whether
or not the allocated money is expended on children, or,
whether that allocation takes into account distributional
concerns, for example, between rural and urban communities or between the poor who need government support
and the not-so-poor who could probably manage without it.

There is then the concept of voice or what, in child rights
circles, is called child participation. This is an important
though complex issue. But, how do we ensure that we have
appropriate indicators to capture the voices of children?
Finally, there is the usual problem of getting the right
statistics and statistics that are comparable and current.
There are weaknesses in this index as is the case with
almost all other similar ones. This means more than any
thing else that we should try to keep on improving this
methodology in order to have a more complete view of the
state of children and measure and compare progress among
governments. This, however, should not detract from the
beauty and power that derive from the simplicity of this
methodology. Much analysis of government obligations is
hampered by the tedious task of having to scan voluminous
information and bulky reports. But this CRC-inspired and
CRC-based methodology provides a simple but powerful,
transparent and objective framework for policy analysis and
comparison and for assessing individual and relative
government performance.

The second important conclusion has to do with the role
of political will and policy in the determination of the state
of and progress in child well-being. Policy-wise, the

experience of child-friendly governments shows the importance of a two-pronged approach to child well-being: (a) adoption and implementation of effective laws and policies; and (b) a policy of child budgeting that prioritises the needs of children.

Finally the African experience confirms what many of us have long suspected. Yes, there are considerable challenges facing governments but progress is possible and feasible even at very low levels of development. You do not have to have oil and diamonds to provide a better country for your children. Rather, success has to do with whether or not children figure in the election manifestoes of politicians and their parties; whether or not they are at the heart of the budgeting process and are given a hearing; whether or not laws are based on the principle of the best interest of the child; whether or not the state has established a child-sensitive juvenile justice system; and whether or not we are moving towards a polity and society that is child-friendly. In other words, are we moving towards good governance? — and this means politics that put children first, laws that protect them, and budgets that provide for them.

⌾

Notes

[1] This essay is based on *The African Report on Child Wellbeing 2008: How Child-friendly are African Governments?* by Assefa Bequclc, Yehualashet Mekonen, David Mugawe, Shimelis Tsegaye and Emma Williams and published by The African Child Policy Forum (ACPF). And so credit for the substance and this summary goes to all of them. All references and sources are from this report. Earlier versions of this essay were presented at the meeting of the African Committee of Experts on the Rights and Welfare of the Child (April 20, 2009) and the Sixth African Conference on Child Abuse and Neglect (May 4, 2009) held in Addis Ababa.

§

References

African Child Policy Forum (ACPF). 2008. *The African Report on Child Wellbeing 2008: How Child-friendly Are African governments?* ACPF, Addis Ababa, Ethiopia.

Ben-Arieh, Asher. 2006. 'Measuring and Monitoring the Wellbeing of Young Children Around the World'. Background paper prepared for the Education for All Global Monitoring Report 2007, Strong Foundations: Early Childhood Care and Education, UNESCO, 2007/ED/EFA/MRT/PI/5, available at http://unesdoc.unesco. org/images/0014/001474/147444e.pdf, accessed on January 5, 2011.

Bradshaw, J., P. Hoelscher and D. Richardson. 2006. 'Child Wellbeing in OECD Countries: Concepts and Methods', Working Paper No. 2006-03, UNICEF Innocenti Research Center, Florence.

Newton, Julie. 2007. 'Structures, Regimes and Wellbeing', WeD Working Paper 30, ESCRC Research Group on Wellbeing in Developing Countries, April, Bath, UK, available at http://www.welldev.org.uk/research/workingpaperpdf/wed30.pdf, accessed on January 5, 2011.

UNICEF. 2006. *Africa's Orphaned and Vulnerable Generations: Affected by AIDS*, UNICEF, New York.

3

Measures to Implement the Convention on the Rights of the Child and Good Governance: The Case of Serbia

Nevena Vuckovic Sahovic

Some Introductory Remarks

State Parties to the Convention on the Rights of the Child (the CRC) are required to undertake all legal, administrative and other measures to implement the rights set forth in the CRC. Introducing the concept of General Measures of Implementation (GMIs) and defining the contents of the measures, the Committee on the Rights of the Child outlined State Parties' obligations in making the CRC a reality. No right of the child can be fully implemented without such measures on every level of governance, including at the level of local communities.

Good governance is characterised by, among other factors, broad societal participation, transparency, accountability, rule of law, effectiveness, equity and refers to the management of government in a manner that is essentially free of abuse and corruption, and with due regard for the rule of law.[1]

While families and the civil society play a very critical role in realising the rights of children, it is important to state at the very outset that it is a primary obligation of the state to implement the CRC, including measures related to justiciability of rights. The organs such as prosecution, or where applicable, social or other services, should make sure those violations of the rights of the child are prevented and attended to. It is the state's obligation to make sure child victims are compensated, rehabilitated and re-integrated into society as well as that perpetrators of violence are brought before justice. While civil society organisations have an extremely critical role to play in the realisation of child rights, it is important that civil society does not take over the role of the state, but that it continues to advocate child-friendly justice to the state.

Using the context of Serbia, a small and young country born in 2006, this chapter aims at identifying elements of good governance in the measures that state parties to the CRC undertake in order to implement rights set forth in that international treaty.[2]

Good Governance and the GMIs

Good governance in the area of the rights of the child is measurable by the level of realisation of those rights. There is a direct and visible relation between good governance and results such as (among others): number of children enrolled into schools, quality of education, quality of services, number of children immunised, number of children placed in institutions or number of children using harmful substances. It is hard to imagine that achieving a high level of realisation of child rights is possible within a governance system that is non-transparent, disorganised, corrupt and non-accountable. In other words, child rights can only be best realised when the state provides for a high level of meaningful participation of all sectors of society, including children and adolescents, in decision-making and implementation of policies, equality, the rule of law and efficiency.

Upon the ratification of the CRC, states undertake an international obligation to ensure the implementation as well as the realisation of human rights for all children under its jurisdiction. The states have committed themselves to undertaking all appropriate legislative, administrative and other measures for the implementation of the rights recognised in the Convention (Article 4 of the CRC). Furthermore, states shall ensure that all domestic legislation is fully compatible with the CRC and that the principles and provisions of the CRC are effectively enforceable. This is a fundamental step. However, all the general measures of implementation have to be addressed. With regard to economic, social and cultural rights, state parties have committed to ensure allocation to the maximum extent of their available resources and, where needed, access resources from within the framework of international cooperation (Article 4 of the CRC).

Although the articles in the CRC lay out the critical area of rights, the Convention does not offer a list of measures. Hence, the Committee on the Rights of the Child (henceforth, the Committee) did so through several documents, such as its Guidelines, Recommendations and General Comments to the Convention. In its first Guidelines for Initial Reporting the Committee identified the 'general measures of implementation' under a specific cluster of Articles 4, 42 (the obligation to make the content of the CRC widely known to children and adults) and Article 44, Paragraph 6 (the obligation to make State Parties' reports widely available within the state).[3] The Committee has clarified its requirements from State Parties in its General Comment No. 5 issued in 2003.[4]

General measures of implementation[5]
- Establishment of child-friendly complaint mechanisms.
- The process of law reform calls on State Parties to ensure the compatibility of existing and new legislation and judicial practice with the Convention.
- Independent national institutions for children's rights need to be developed — such as children's ombudsmen offices, child rights commissioners and focal points within national human rights institutions.
- Comprehensive national agendas or strategies for implementation of the Convention are needed.

- Child rights-focused permanent institutions and structures within government are required to ensure coordination and pursue implementation.
- On-going data collection and research.
- Allocation of resources to children 'to the maximum extent of their availability' is key in State Parties' efforts to ensure implementation.
- Systematic monitoring of the implementation of the CRC is needed through effective child-related data collection, analysis, evaluation and dissemination.
- Education, training and awareness-raising on children's rights need to be promoted.
- The involvement of civil society, including children, is critical if there is to be progress on implementation.
- International cooperation.

Human rights, including rights of the child are indivisible and hence no right can be realised in isolation of others. As with child rights as a whole, the general measures to implement those rights are also indivisible, interdependent and closely interrelated. In other words, their implementation is mutually supportive. Therefore, the specification of the general measures is grounded in a full understanding of the spirit and intent of the CRC. As the Committee has stressed in its Reporting Guidelines, equal importance needs to be attached to each and every right recognised by the CRC.[6] The general measures of implementation identified by the Committee are intended to promote full enjoyment by all children, of all rights recognised by the CRC.

In line with the principle of indivisibility, it is important to consider the role and impact of all sectors of society in the implementation of all the general measures. However, the State Party remains the main duty bearer of all international obligations, including those to undertake all measures to make the rights of the child a reality. In the CRC's Article 12, it is clearly stated that due weight should be given to children's views in all matters affecting them. Involving all sectors of society, including children themselves, parents and wider families, other adults, and non-state services and organisations, goes beyond the implementation of the CRC. It is a governance issue and a reflection of democracy.

There are various ways of implementing the Convention and there are no magic solutions. The measures to implement child rights vary from country to country and the results are always more visible where and when they are carried out within a more successful governance setting. During 20 years of the implementation of the CRC, many State Parties to this treaty have undergone profound reforms and have been through difficult or successful times.[7]

Serbia is bordered by Hungary to the north; Romania and Bulgaria to the east; the Republic of Macedonia and Albania to the south; and Croatia, Bosnia and Herzegovina and Montenegro to the west. Serbia is militarily neutral and awaiting accession to the European Union (EU).

Serbia, a federal part of Yugoslavia after World War II, became an independent state in 2006. As Yugoslavia broke up in the 1990s, Serbia remained in a union with Montenegro until 2006, when Montenegro opted for separation. From 1991 to 2010 numerous and enormous social changes occurred. The implementation of the CRC in Serbia, as indeed in many other countries of south-eastern Europe, needs to be seen in the difficult context of consequences of the wars in the region in the 1990s, transition from socialist to market economy and the European Union accession process. The political and economic crisis in the region had resulted in the deterioration, and in some cases collapse, of the social protection structures in the region. Social security, health, education and cultural activities had suffered as a result of the shift of priority towards other sectors, seriously hampering the realisation of the rights of the child.

General context in Serbia

Serbia today:

Basic facts:

- Territory: 88,361 km²
- Number of municipalities: 160
- Population: 7,463,157
- Ethnic composition:
  - Serbs: 6,212,838
  - Roma: 108,193
  - Hungarian: 293,299
  - Bosnian: 136,087
  - Albanian: 61,674
  - Montenegrin: 69,049
- Children (under 19 years of age): 1,662,029 (22.27%)
- GDP per capita: US$ 4,028
- Inflation in 2007: 9.7%
- Average net salary: approximately 400 USD

*Source: Implementation of the convention on the rights of the child in
Serbia. Prepared by the coalition of non-governmental organi-
sations in Serbia under the coordination of the Child Rights
Centre, Belgrade, Serbia, December 2007.*

In addition to these general problems affecting the region, Serbia was, due to political reasons (undemocratic regime in conflict with most of the major international actors), in total isolation from the rest of the world. Serbia was between 1992 and 2000 neither a member of the UN nor of any other system within the international community. It was even excluded from all sport competitions and many artistic competitions and events during that period. In 1993, Serbia had the highest inflation rate ever recorded in the history of the world during which the average monthly wage was 2 Deutsch Marks. In 1998 the conflicts in its province of Kosovo and Metohija culminated and ended in an international intervention and a three-month bombing of Serbia in the spring of 1999.

The Current Situation of Children in Serbia as of 2006

The economic, political and social improvement of the last decade has brought fundamental political changes. In June 2006 the State Union of Serbia and Montenegro was dissolved. For the first time in nearly 90 years Serbia is an independent country. However, it is unsettling that unsatisfactory cooperation with the war crimes tribunal for the former Yugoslavia in The Hague is slowing down the EU accession negotiation processes. The unresolved status of Kosovo is another significant political problem of Serbia. The current political situation in Serbia is characterised by a struggling coalition government, still inadequate rule of law, a high degree of corruption and a slow decentralisation process.[8] Needless to say all this has an impact on the realisation of the rights of children in the country, which is reflected on their situation. A large number of children in Serbia still live in poverty. Persistent political problems shift focus from the economic issues and stall reforms. Two major problems are unemployment and low levels of productivity. Due to an increase in the real cost of living, a large number of families are not able to bring up their children properly and ensure quality education for them.

Violence against children is a problem in Serbia and it is committed in all five contexts of the UN Study on Violence—school, family, institutions, local environment and work place—mostly by adults.[9] The attitude towards violence against children, particularly in schools and families, is still very conservative. Corporal punishment, for example, is still an acceptable form of disciplining children in families and it is still widely used in schools, where it is forbidden, and in institutions and residential care settings. Children are too often subject to different forms of degrading treatments and punishments. An increase and change in the nature of peer violence is particularly disconcerting.

Most important results achieved:

- In 2006 a new constitution was adopted, one that for the first time in the constitutional history of Serbia has specific child rights provisions.
- A number of important laws were passed:
  - ❏ Family law (2005)
  - ❏ Law on juvenile offenders and criminal justice for juveniles (2005, in practice since January 1, 2006)
  - ❏ Criminal Code (2005, in practice since January 1, 2006)
  - ❏ Law on the basics of the education system (2003, amended 2004)
  - ❏ Law on protection of persons with disabilities from discrimination (2006)
- Numerous strategies with the aim of improving the state of child rights in Serbia were approved:
  - ❏ National Action Plan
  - ❏ Rights of persons with disabilities
  - ❏ Protection of children from abuse and neglect
  - ❏ Protection of children from exploitation
  - ❏ Protection of children from human trafficking
  - ❏ Inclusion of Roma children
- Institutional mechanisms set up for the development of child rights:
  - ❏ Establishment and development of the Child Rights Council as the advisory interdepartmental body
  - ❏ Appointment of a Serbian human rights deputy ombudsman in charge of child rights
  - ❏ Establishment of the Department of Child Rights Ombudsman affiliated to the regional Vojvodina Ombudsman
  - ❏ Submission of the initial report on the implementation of the Child Rights Convention in Serbia
  - ❏ Establishment of the Working Group to draft Child Rights Act (under the auspices of the Deputy Ombudsman for Child Rights)

Challenges that Remain:

- Improvement of the law reform — adoption of a Child Rights Act
- Decrease in the number of children living in poverty

- Increasing and specification of budget allocation for children
- A higher level of political interest, knowledge and attention towards children
- Fundamental reform of the education system, in accordance with international standards
- The improvement of health care for children, including adolescent health
- A higher level of education and information dissemination on child rights, in as a broad as possible spectrum of beneficiaries, in particular, children, their parents, teachers and health workers
- Facilitation of an efficient child protection system (emergency interventions) from all forms of abuse and exploitation, including ones in the context of trafficking, occurring through media and availability of harmful information on the internet

General Measures to Implement the CRC and the Progress in Serbia

◈

Law Reform

The new constitution of the Republic of Serbia, adopted in 2006, includes for the first time in the constitutional history of the country a provision devoted explicitly to child rights. The constitution prescribes that child rights are to be regulated by law, but an important opportunity was missed by not proclaiming the basic principles of the Convention as constitutional principles. International treaties are directly implemented in the Republic of Serbia. Judiciary and administrative bodies more and more implement international regulations, although this information is not based on a regular collection of information.

The process of law reform based on the ratification of international law, calls on States Parties to ensure compatibility of existing and new legislation and judicial practice with the CRC, in a number of ways, including: through comprehensive reviews of legislation; the inclusion of children's rights in the Constitution; the development of specific laws to reflect the CRC principles and provisions; responding to 'new' issues related to children's rights; and considering effective remedies for children and their representatives if children's rights are violated.

Although states may agree in principle, the introduction of new solutions is slow and not always succeeded by thorough development of implementation mechanisms. In Serbia, national laws are not fully harmonised with the Convention and other international human rights instruments. The endeavour of drafting the Child Rights Act is an encouraging process and if successful, will, by 2011, ensure full harmonisation of national laws with international standards, in particular with the CRC.

The legal remedy system in Serbia does not include the prescence of children in all instances when child issues are being decided upon, because the child does not have the status of party to proceedings, which is a consequence of imprecisely defined child participation (i.e., an inadequately resolved procedural position of the child in proceedings under family law, as a consequence of the unattended issue of independent legal representation of children in all court and administrative proceedings that concern the child).

Needless to say, justiciability of child rights remains a pending issue in Serbia, like in many State Parties to the CRC. The organs such as prosecution, or where applicable, social or other services, should make sure that violation of the rights of the child are prevented and attended to. It is the state's obligation to make sure child victims are compensated, rehabilitated and re-integrated into society, as well as that perpetrators of violence are brought before justice.

The child rights protection mechanism in the Republic of Serbia provides for the possibility of regular and ad hoc legal remedies including appealing to the constitutional court of Serbia. Furthermore, keeping in mind that Serbia is a member of the Council of Europe there is the option of submitting applications to the European Human Rights Court in Strasbourg, when all legal remedies provided by the domestic legal system are exhausted.

◊

National Strategies/Plans of Action for Children

In its General Comment No. 5, the Committee on the Rights of the Child sent a clear message to governments that in order to make children's rights a reality they needed to work on the basis of a unifying, comprehensive and rights-based national strategy, based on the CRC. A comprehensive strategy or national plan of action for children should take into account the recommendations given in the concluding observations by the Committee upon examination of state reports. It should be developed through a process of consultation, including with children and young people and those living and working with them. To give the strategy authority, it should be endorsed at the highest level of government, be linked to national development planning and included in national budgeting; it must include a description of a sustainable process for realising the rights of children throughout the state; it must set real and achievable targets in relation to the full range of rights for all children.[10]

Governments may decide to develop a comprehensive national plan or sectoral plans of action—for example, for juvenile justice or internet safety—which set out specific goals, targeted implementation measures and allocation of financial and human resources, but not with the intention to replace a comprehensive national strategy. The strategy has to be adequately resourced, in human and financial terms, and be coordinated with all the other sectoral national plans. Developing a national strategy is a more permanent and comprehensive process that includes identification of arrangements for monitoring and continuous review, for regular updating and for periodic reports to parliament and to the public.

The basis for all activities that the Republic of Serbia undertakes towards improving the state of child rights in the country is the National Action Plan for children that was adopted in 2004, and which includes guidelines necessary for the improvement of the status of the child, in other words, define directions for development in various areas. While the National Action Plan for Children does not represent an overall national strategy because it does not focus on all child rights, it provides some basis for the improvement of the state of child rights. However, years after its adoption, especially in the area of child health and the status of children with disabilities, no important improvements are noted. Little has been done in the area of education, and in the area of protection of children without parental care. Only the reduction of poverty has been thoroughly put in motion—through the Strategy for Poverty Reduction. Expected results have not been achieved so far.

The Serbian National Action Plan for Children has been the basis for designing Local Action Plans at municipal levels. Sixteen local action plans were developed in 2007, but they are not being thoroughly implemented in some municipalities because funds for their realisation have not been clearly allocated. In 2007 another five towns began designing Local Action Plans for children. Unfortunately the three largest cities in Serbia — Belgrade, Novi Sad and Nis, were not among them.[11]

◊

State Coordination

The implementation of the CRC cannot be successful unless there is government accountability and coordination and convergence between the national and the local governments, ministries and departments. Many times, child rights issues are dealt with by a particular governmental department, or scattered over different departments, but without adequate coordination or no coordination at all. Ideally, every state should have a specific coordination and monitoring body for children, at a central and in strategic position within the government. The purpose of such a body is to make children visible in government's action, ensure the coordination of relevant activities, to monitor progress and promote a comprehensive and integrated agenda for the realisation of children's rights.

In the context of the Republic of Serbia, the main body tasked with the implementation of the CRC, that is, activities in the field of child rights, is the Child Rights Council, formed in 2002. In the initial years of its existence, the Council was affected by personnel changes, etc. in the government. The institutional reforms of the Council which took place during 2005 and 2006 addressed some of the weaknesses and made the work of this body less dependent on personnel changes in the government. However, the formation of the Council is not backed by a law and despite the institutional changes it has undergone, the coordinating role of the Council has not been properly realised, nor has it been adequately resourced with finances and trained staff.

Except for the Council, mechanisms of intersectional cooperation in Serbia have not been introduced and there is lack of adequate coordination between relevant subsystems—education, social protection, justice, finance, health care and internal affairs. Coordination between national government and local administration is either poor or non-existent, which is the main obstacle for coordinated activities at the central and local level.

Child welfare in general is not given specific and sincere attention, mainly due to political interests of a multiparty coalition within the government and their constant bargaining, including in the most important areas of child rights such as health or education.

Budgeting for Child Rights

An essential question in democracies is how the state resources are distributed. It is often one of the topics that generate hot debates in parliaments, across governments and among the general public. In its General Comment No. 5, the Committee emphasised that governments should take steps 'to ensure that economic and social planning and decision-making and budgetary decisions are made with the best interests of children as a primary consideration and that children, including in particular marginalized and disadvantaged groups of children, are protected from the adverse effects of economic policies or financial downturns'.[12]

Budget allocations in the Republic of Serbia are allocated through ministries in charge of social policy and education; it is difficult to disaggregate spending by age groups. This makes it difficult to analyse how much resources are intended for children and where these funds are directed. Lack of transparency and the lack of a disaggregated system of accounting make it impossible to identify budget allocations for children.

For a number of years Serbia has allocated between 3.5 and 3.8 per cent of GDP for education, which is considered very low (this places Serbia at the bottom of the European list of states spending on education). GDP percentage that is intended for social transfers is constantly around 1.4 per cent, which also is the lowest in the region.

◊

Data Collection and Research

There can be no successful implementation of children's rights without knowledge of the situation of children as it exists. This can be achieved only through collection of reliable data and their thorough assessment. Without such data, no adequate planning and monitoring is possible. The State Parties to the CRC should always make sure that in-depth studies are undertaken on issues covered by the treaty and that a uniform information system that ensures that disaggregated data, *inter alia* by age, sex, disability and ethnic or social origin is systematically collected and analysed. Such activities are essential tools for assessment, policy development and implementation. Traditionally, data is collected by government departments, research institutes and universities. However, civil society organisations also carry out a lot of research and data collection, alone or in cooperation with other institutions, including with international organisations such as UNICEF.

The National Plan of Action (NPA) for children in Serbia envisages improvements in the development of indicators and DevINFO, a database system for monitoring human development and a tool for organising, storing and presenting data.[13] Consequently, indicators for monitoring were developed as a part of the defined goals and tasks of the NPA. Yet there is still no data on a number of child-related issues. The existing data and statistics are not regularly updated. On the other hand, the concept of the data base in theory allows data collection by municipalities, which often leads to discrepancies. The Statistical Office of the Republic of Serbia gathers data of general interest which is the basis for analysis of other indicators, but in doing so it does not use the 18 years age limit to disaggregate data for children and adults. Consequently there is no accurate data on the number of persons younger than 18 years of age. Data that refers to individual areas are gathered partially and are complicated because of different methodological approaches.

◊

Monitoring the Implementation

Monitoring of the implementation of the CRC is one of the most important general measures of implementation. Every

State Party to the CRC should regularly monitor the implementation, in an organised and planned manner. Yet, it is important that there is an independent opinion on the states' actions in child rights. And yes, it is one of the states' obligations to support such independent monitoring, since it greatly contributes to good governance.

Across the world, international organisations, states, national bodies and local organisations, all undertake monitoring of the implementation of the CRC and realisation of child rights. The implementation of the CRC is not possible without independent monitoring which is carried out by national human rights institutions, civil society or international governmental organisations. Independent monitoring generates action for advocacy, governments' and other actors' actions. Monitoring results are used to provide advice on gaps and measures needed to fulfil children's rights.

The concept of National Human Rights Institutions (NHRIs) for children has been developed within the framework of Article 4 of the CRC, and was further elaborated in the Committee's General Comment No. 2 on the Role of Independent NHRIs in the Promotion and Protection of the Rights of the Child.[14] Independent human rights institutions for children are different from NGOs in that they are public institutions, based on legislation, financed by state budget and report to the parliament and/ or government. Independent institutions for children's rights have multiplied in all regions and are present in many countries around the world.

State monitoring mechanisms in Serbia are still insufficiently developed and they rest within the boundaries of habitual supervision of everyday activities within the government departments (administrative oversight) and judicial control of administrative and judicial acts (second-degree decision-making in judicial proceedings). However, the work of the deputy human rights ombudsman, who is in charge of the Rights of the Child, has developed well since the establishment of this office in 2007. The office of the deputy receives complaints and monitors the work of administrative organs. It has significant public authority and respect. It also has legal power to initiate a law reform procedure, hence it has established a Working Group for the Drafting of the Child Rights Act in Serbia.

◇

Training and Education

Twenty years after the adoption of the CRC it is clear that understanding child rights is the key to their full realisation. Therefore, awareness raising, training and education are crucial to the implementation of the CRC and all other measures. The process of implementation of the CRC calls on state parties, professionals working with children, parents and children and other stakeholders to steadily carry out education, training and awareness-raising on children's rights. The universal and speedy ratification of the CRC was surprising taking into account diversities in understanding childhoods and rights. In the process of implementation of child rights there are still tensions and conflicts, mostly due to values and attitudes. Such tensions are based on the lack of knowledge and information and are one of the biggest obstacles to the implementation of the CRC.

At the beginning of this decade, as part of the initiated reform of the educational system in Serbia, the intention was to introduce the Convention to the children through the educational system. However, this idea did not go through as intended. Children are at present introduced to the Convention in school through the subject Civic Education. This subject is optional. Children who do not opt for this subject, unfortunately, cannot be introduced to the Convention during other classes. In the mean time, training of civic education teachers became scattered, thus resulting in a decrease in professional capacity for teaching the subject. When speaking about dissemination and introducing of the Convention to the parents, the state has not taken any steps towards this aim.

Most of the training and education on child rights in Serbia are organised and carried out by NGOs, with the assistance of international organisations. Professionals working with children such as family law judges have to go through obligatory education in the area of child rights. The same goes for professionals of the Justice Ministry and the Ministry of the Interior working on the juvenile justice system, as well as representatives of the Bar Association. Unfortunately, this kind of education is limited in time and therefore in scope and does not result in change of attitudes and gain of profound knowledge in child rights. One bright example is Master in Child Rights at the Belgrade-based Union Faculty of Law, introduced as of 2007.

◇

Cooperation with the Civil Society/NGOs

Civil society operates in a world which is run by governments. National and international NGOs often depend on and cooperate with governments. In most of the countries, NGOs which deal with child rights either cooperate or cohabitate peacefully with their governments. Often governments formally recognise the important role played by non-governmental organisations (NGOs) in carrying out, monitoring and evaluating child rights-related programmes.

Unfortunately, however, state authorities in Serbia, especially ministries, still do not recognise the NGO sector as a full-fledged partner. During 2007 certain improvements were made and the process of strengthening cooperation was initiated. The Vice Premiers Team for the Implementation of the Strategy for Reduction of Poverty introduced a programme of cooperation with civil society organisations, financed by the International Development Department of the United Kingdom. Contact organisations were chosen for seven sensitive groups, including children who facilitated communication channels and cooperation of organisations dealing with child rights. In all ministries (except in the Ministry for Education) contact persons for cooperation with the organisations were appointed. However, there continues to be a lack of transparency in that cooperation. The government has not introduced and published clear criteria for cooperation with NGOs.

The situation is rather satisfactory in implementation of the programmes and projects. The government is open to cooperate with NGOs in legislative reforms, transformation of social system institutions and in areas which need further training and education. As long as NGOs provide funding for child rights activities, the state organs in Serbia willingly cooperate.

◈

International Cooperation

Much of the work on the implementation of the CRC was possible due to international cooperation. In its General Comment No. 5, the Committee states that 'Article 4 emphasizes that implementation of the Convention is a cooperative exercise for the States of the world. This article and others in the Convention highlight the need for international cooperation.'[15] The overall Committee message regarding international cooperation is that the CRC should form the framework for international cooperation and be rights-based and that State Parties which receive international assistance should allocate a substantive part of that aid specifically earmarked for children. Such an approach requires that 'Governments, donors and civil society ensure that children are a prominent priority in the development of PRSPs and sector wide approaches to development'.[16]

International organisations that deal with child issues (UNICEF, Save the Children, Agency for Reconstruction, World Bank and others) have a twofold role in Serbia: some of them are active in project and programme implementation (UNICEF, Save the Children) and provide financial, logistical and human resource aid to local NGOs and state agencies, while others generally finance reforms that are carried out within state structures (Agency for Reconstruction, World Bank). Thanks to their assistance most of the achievements in the implementation of the Convention were made possible.

Conclusions

There are many challenges to the exercise of the rights of the child and it is of utmost importance to address them in an integrated and interrelated manner. General measures, good governance, national as well as international factors all influence implementation of child rights and actual exercise of child rights. Serbia has not fully put in place all measures to implement child rights. On the other hand, Serbia still suffers economic, social and political downfalls which seriously impede its ability to fulfil the obligation to ensure that all elements of good governance are in place in the country. Those factors are clearly internal, but they are also related to international and global issues. The global economic crisis has not by-passed Serbia and has gravely affected its fragile economy. Financial downturns and crisis always impact the well-being of children, and this is what happened in Serbia as well. UNICEF views the current global economic crisis as threatening to reverse accomplishments in child survival and well-being: 'Countries on track to meet the Millennium Development Goals could fall behind, while those that were struggling to advance could be left even worse off. The crisis threatens both the resources of families as well as national budgets, creating serious challenges to the fulfillment of children's and women's rights.'[17] It is not clear to what extent Serbian politics and strategies prioritise or even take into account children. Politicians in Serbia still address voters rather than groups whose members do not guarantee their stay in power, such as children or refugees.

Environmental issues, such as climate change, extreme pollution and land degradation seriously impede joint efforts to make child rights a reality. Natural disasters often come with no warning and hit even the most economically advanced countries and regions. Serbia experiences floods and landslides due to man-made causes, but also because of natural factors which go beyond the states' borders. Children, in particular those living in poverty, are the most vulnerable victims of such disasters.

Due to the growth in information technology, children in Serbia, as elsewhere, are more exposed to direct and indirect violence, in particular through the internet. Security issues related to crime and violence, internal and international illegal activities threaten children in Serbia. As in many parts of the world, in spite of enormous efforts of all stakeholders in all parts of the world to prevent and protect children, it remains a great challenge to implement the CRC in such circumstances.

Finally, in relation to good governance there is a lack of political commitment and continuity in the implementation of measures in many State Parties to the CRC, and Serbia is no exception. Children do not benefit from just procedures for justification of their rights. Children in Serbia are still victims of discrimination on various grounds and one of the biggest challenges throughout the government is to pay full attention to equity and inclusiveness. The disparities are increasing and there is a general impression among the population that no one is accountable for such a situation. Effective and efficient governance remains fundamental for the implementation of child rights in Serbia and no measure to implement those rights can be successful unless it is improved. It is fair to acknowledge all the efforts in Serbia in the last 20 years to implement the CRC, in particular taking into account the factors mentioned here and the difficulties that have impeded realisation of child rights, as well as acknowledge the results. But it is important to note that more could have been done, and more has to be done, keeping in mind that the realisation of child rights is the paramount obligation of the government. Civil society or international community can advocate and contribute to installation of good governance and can assist measures but a significant result can be achieved only when and where there is political will and action. Children in Serbia are still waiting.

✄

Notes

[1] See http://stats.oecd.org/glossary/detail.asp?ID=7237, accessed on March 17, 2011.

[2] Serbia is a south-eastern European country and was part of the former federal republic of Yugoslavia.

[3] General guidelines regarding the form and content of initial reports to be submitted by State Parties under Article 44, Paragraph 1(a), of the Convention: October 30, 1991, CRC/C/5.

[4] UN Committee on the Rights of the Child. General measures of implementation of the Convention on the Rights of the Child (Articles 4, 42 and 44, Para. 6), CRC/GC/2003/5, 2003.

[5] It was one of the major commitments of the states within the follow-up process to the 1990 World Summit for Children and the 2002 United Nations General Assembly Special Session on Children.

[6] 'The provisions of the Convention have been grouped under different sections, equal importance being attached to all the rights recognized by the Convention.' Paragraph 8 of the General Guidelines regarding the form and content of initial

reports to be submitted by States Parties under Article 44, Paragraph 1(a), of the Convention, CRC/C/5, 1991.

'The present guidelines group the articles of the Convention in clusters with a view to assisting States Parties in the preparation of their reports. This approach reflects the holistic perspective on children's rights taken by the Convention: i.e. that they are indivisible and interrelated, and that equal importance should be attached to each and every right recognized therein.' Paragraph 3 of the General Guidelines regarding the form and the content of periodic reports to be submitted by State Parties under Article 44, Paragraph 1(B) of the Convention, 2005.

[7] One hundred and ninety-three states have ratified the CRC and the remaining two have signed (USA and Somalia).

[8] For more information on Serbia, please visit the web page of the Child Rights Centre Belgrade, www.cpd.org.rs, accessed on March 17, 2011.

[9] See http://www2.ohchr.org/english/bodies/crc/study.htm, accessed on March 17, 2011.

[10] UN Committee on the Rights of the Child. General measures of implementation of the Convention on the Rights of the Child (Articles 4, 42 and 44, Para 6), 2003, Paragraphs 71–79.

[11] Uzice is the first town in Serbia that adopted a strategy for children. The municipal parliament approved the document in 2005. It is a strategic text that is fully in accordance with NPA and the Poverty Reduction Strategy (PRSP) and was created as a result of local capacities and the NGO sector lobbying the local government to begin this process, especially the Uzice Child Rights Centre. Uzice municipality allocated 18,000 USD from the local budget for the implementation of the strategy for children, 36,000 USD in 2006 and over 90,000 in 2007. In the Pirot municipal budget 14,500 USD was allocated for the implementation of the Local Plan of Action (LPA). In 2007 they significantly increased the financing to 36,000 USD.

[12] UN Committee on the Rights of the Child. General Comment No. 5 (2003): General measures of implementation of the Convention on the Rights of the Child (Articles 4, 42 and 44, Para 6), 2003, Para 51.

[13] See www.devinfo.org, accessed on March 17, 2011.

2221222221121222132232221122222222

[14] UN Committee on The Rights of The Child. General Comment No. 2. (2002), The role of independent national human rights institutions in the promotion and protection of the rights of the child. Thirty-second session. January 13–31, 2003, CRC/GC/2002/2, November 15, 2002.

[15] UN Committee on the Rights of the Child, General Comment No. 5, 2003, General measures of implementation of the Convention on the Rights of the Child (Articles 4, 42 and 44, Para 6), 2003, Para 60.

[16] Ibid.

[17] See http://www.unicef.org/socialpolicy/index_49070.html, accessed on June 2, 2010.

References

Belgrade Centre for Human Rights. 2007. *Human Rights in Serbia 2006*, Belgrade.

Brkic, M., V. Cucic, V. Dejanovic, L. Jovanovic, V. Jovanovic, D. Kozic, N. Milosevic, L. Pejakovic, M. Pesic, A. Ramah, D. Stanimirovic, I. Stevanovic, O. Vidojevic, S. Vorkapic, N. Vuckovic Sahovic and D. Vulevic. 2003. *Child Rights in Serbia 1996–2000* (Serbian and English), Child Rights Centre, Belgrade.

Child Rights in Serbia 2003—General Context. 2004. Belgrade (English).

Cucic, V., V. Dejanovic, V. Jovanovic, L. Pejakovic, M. Pesic, V. Rajovic, M. Sretenovic, I. Stevanovic, S. Vorkapic, N. Vuckovic Sahovic, R. Vujovic and D. Vulevic. 2004. *Child Rights in Serbia 2003* (Serbian), Child Rights Centre, Belgrade.

General Measures of Implementation of the Convention on the Rights of the Child. 2006. UNICEF Innocenti Research Centre, Florence.

Implementation Handbook for the Convention on the Rights of the Child. 2002. UNICEF, New York.

Petrovic, Marija, Nevena Vuckovic Sahovic and Ivana Stevanovic. 2004. *National Plan of Action for Children, Republic of Serbia* (Internet Wikipedia), Belgrade.

————. 2006. *Child Rights in Serbia 2005* (Serbian, Summary in English), Child Rights Centre, Belgrade.

Nevena Vuckovic Sahovic. 2007. *Child Rights in Serbia 2006*, Child Rights Centre, Belgrade.

Save the Children Sweden. 2007. *Child Rights Monitoring at Local Level*.

UN Country team. 2003. *Common Country Assessment for Serbia and Montenegro*, Belgrade.

Vorkapic, Sladjana, Nevena Vuckovic Sahovic, Vesna Dejanovic, Tanja Zogovic, Mirjana Pesic, Ivana Stevanovic, Oliver Toskovic, Ljubomir Pejakovic and Viktorija Cucic. 2005. *Child Rights in Serbia 2004* (Serbian and English), Child Rights Centre, Belgrade.

Yugoslav Child Rights Centre Volume. 1999. *Bulletin. Newsletter of the Yugoslav Child Rights Centre Volume III*, Numbers 9 & 10, December, Belgrade.

4

A Story of Neglect: Children in Peru's Public Budgets

Enrique Vásquez

Introduction

Peru has a long tradition of neglecting poorer children; the reason offered being lack of resources. Public policy requires greater targeted attention towards this vulnerable group. Legal commitment must be matched with financial commitments.

The budget of any country showcases the government's true priorities vis-à-vis planned expenditure. The UN convention on the Rights of the Child states that 'State parties shall undertake such measures to the maximum extent of available resources and where needed the framework of international cooperation' (Article 4). Expanding on this, the UN Committee on the Rights of the Child, in its General Comment on General Measures of Implementation for the Rights of the Child, has said, 'Whatever their economic circumstances, States are required to undertake all possible measures towards the realisation of the rights of the child, paying special attention to the most disadvantaged groups' (Para 8). It adds, 'Implementation of the human rights of children must not be seen as a charitable process, bestowing favours on children' (Para 11) (General Comment No. 5 on General Measures of Implementation for the Convention on the Rights of the Child, 2003). It is in this context that it becomes imperative to monitor the budgets of any country, and how far it has been effective in addressing the needs of its children.

This essay shares empirical evidence from Peru on the need for an independent monitoring and evaluating system for all kinds of spending on children. International experience shows that over time, such spending systems can get entrenched and immune to change, even influenced by political elements. An evaluation system within agencies discourages effort, affecting the quality of the results and the information collected.

Using efficacy, efficiency, equity and transparency as the four pillars of public administration, this essay discusses the state of affairs in Peru. It also shares the methodology that was used to monitor public spending in programmes for children, using Cuentas's (2005) six stages of successful implementation, and discusses the role of data collection and databases, and the need for specially designed and refined monitoring and evaluation systems, and the lessons learnt through this exercise. The essay draws upon the experience of an initiative to reduce the gender gap in education to illustrate the methodology for evaluating the state's compliance of rights commitments to children.

Public Spending and Children

In Peru, the track record of governments in management of public resources aimed at reducing poverty has been poor. Differences between planned and actual spending, a tendency towards regressive public spending, leakage and poor coverage in social programmes and lack of coordination among public institutions are the characteristics of such mismanagement during the past decade. Between 1990 and 2000, public social spending went up from $11 million to $1,500 million.[1] Poverty levels went down initially from 57.4 per cent in 1991 to 50.7 per cent in 1997, only to rise again to 54.1 per cent in 2001 (ENNIV 2000). In fact, throughout the 1990s, public social spending matched the GDP curve. In other words, in times of economic slowdown, the most vulnerable groups were left unattended due to low growth and a lack of resources.

Inequalities persisted between rural and urban areas, as public social spending did not reach the low-income households and the excluded geographic regions (ibid.).

Leakage occurs when a person who is not part of the targeted population is classified as one and is included in a programme. Under-coverage occurs when a person is part of the goal population and his or her access to a public programme is denied. Both errors are inefficient and inconvenient. On one side, leakage wastes programme resources because the amount designated for poor (especially children) is smaller or because it is necessary to increase the budget required to obtain the same impact. And on the other hand, under-coverage leaves the most vulnerable without assistance (Monge et al. 2009). Those problems occur because the officials have inadequate information to identify the vulnerable population. To achieve a level of accuracy in information gathering it is necessary to invest in administrative costs (ibid.).

A study on the relationship of public spending and rights of children requires:
(a) a methodology of construction and processing of budgetary statistics so that federal and local agencies could view this vulnerable group as well as the risks to which they are exposed
(b) statistical results of monitoring of the efficiency and efficacy of all public resources aimed at the children
(c) a system that allows for generating and processing information to check if the state commitments with regard to children's rights have been kept.

Figure 4.1 shows the sector-wise distribution of public social spending from 2005 to 2009. The major proportion of public social spending has been allocated to education, followed by the health sector. However, the impact of this spending is not reflected in the coverage rate.

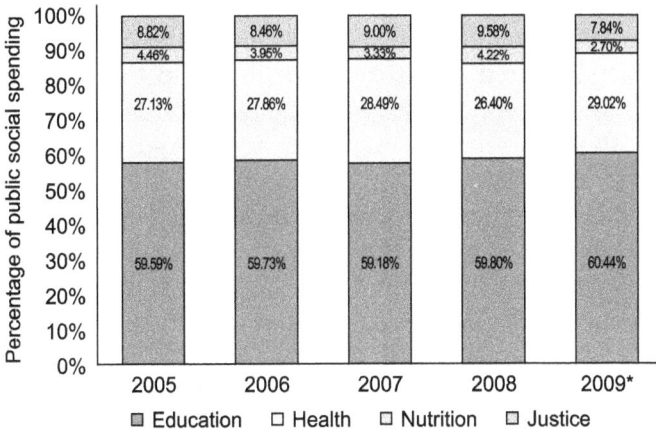

*The nutrition rubric includes just the budget assigned to Programa Nacional de Asistencia Alimentaria-Pronaa, September 2009

Source: MEF/SIAF/PRONAA
Elaboration: Centro de Investigación de la Universidad del Pacífico (CIUP)

Fig. 4.1: *Distribution of Public Social Spending by Sectors in Peru: 2005–09**

In the health sector, the 1990s saw some significant achievements in terms of access and quality of health services for children. While chronic malnutrition dropped by a third from 34 per cent in 1990 to 22.9 per cent in 2000, the urban–rural disparities remained with 50 per cent of the public spending in child health concentrated in more affluent geographical areas like Lima and Callao whereas in Huancavelica and Ayacucho, where more than 90 per cent of the households are very poor, it is extremely inadequate (Vásquez 2005a). With public social spending not reaching the low-income households, the persisting inequalities between rural and urban areas get reflected in the health status (Vásquez and Mendizábal 2003). The malnutrition ratio for children below five years in the rural provinces was a higher 4:10 (or 40 per cent) compared to only 1:10 (or 10 per cent) in urban areas (INEI 2000) and chronic malnutrition rates in rural areas in the Andean and Amazon regions remained static at 40 per cent and 32.4 per cent respectively (ibid.). With the rural–urban and rich–poor gaps maintained, one out of every four children (or 25 per cent of all children) in Peru remained chronically malnourished even in 2000.

It was a similar story with malnourished children in school-going age; while their national share dropped by 10 points from 39.1 per cent to 29.8 per cent, in rural areas that share was still a large 48.5 per cent in 2000 (Censo de 1993 and Censo Nacional de Talla en Escolares 1999). To make matters worse, the nutrition programmes recorded a high degree of leakage—45.2 per cent of the beneficiaries didn't belong to the target group of a given programme—as well as under-coverage: they didn't reach 84.6 per cent of the target group (Vásquez and Monge 2007).

While the child mortality rates went down significantly from 81.7 per thousand live births in 1990 in rural areas to 53 per thousand in 1999, the decline was much sharper— to 27.2 per thousand—in urban areas (ibid.).

The state of education in Peru too shows that it remains a major barrier to sustainable development with approximately 7 per cent of the children and adolescents under 18 years not attending school, 33 per cent of whom are poor and 35 per cent are extremely poor (Vásquez 2009). Further, the 1990s saw little improvement in the level and quality of basic regular education, especially in rural areas, although dropout and failure rates have reduced (Yamada 2007). Returns from investment in education over time diminished in the case of primary education to 5.6 per cent for incomplete primary and 3.8 per cent for completed primary education in 2004 (ENAHO 2004), compared to 9.1 per cent and 4.2 per cent respectively (ENNIV 2000) in 1994. Secondary education fared worse, with enrollments becoming half from what they were in the 1980s, to 5.1 per cent for incomplete secondary and 6.3 per cent for complete secondary. In 1985, these numbers were 10.5 per cent and 13.1 per cent (ENNIV 2000). In the case of higher education too, the enrollment diminished, to 10.8 per cent in 2004 (ENAHO 2004), though college education returns have soared about 40 per cent from the 1980s to 12.7 per cent and 17.3 per cent (ENAHO 2004).

Investment return rates for basic education are low in Peru for several reasons. A major cause is completing primary or secondary school does not provide a family the extra income that it feels would justify investment in the child's education (Vásquez 2009). This should compel the government to consider adequate incentives to schooling, though we do not concern ourselves with that here. This study, on the contrary, highlights the shortcomings of a public education system that does not invest in teacher development or teacher evaluation.

The Principles of Public Budgeting

Every state committed to respect children's rights, in terms of access to health, sanitation, education, nutrition, justice and welfare, should have an organisation structure that ensures such rights are upheld at both national and municipal levels. The public administration body should be founded on four basic principles: efficacy, efficiency, equity and transparency. In other words, it should pursue a result-oriented public budget based on budgetary links, administrative expenses that are 10 per cent or less of programme costs, and proper utilisation of the entire funds allocated to programmes, projects and activities for children and teenagers.[2]

Efficacy: implies the achievement of the programme goals within projected timeframes and quality levels. There are two indicators that allow identifying the degree of equality with which programmes are designed and developed: the rate of under-coverage or the percentage share of the target population that is not reached, and the rate of filtration or the share of people reached that do not belong to the target population.

Peru's nutritional programmes are plagued by leakage and under-coverage. In regions where the number of beneficiaries is low, almost half of the beneficiaries are those who should not have been the targets. Under-coverage, on the contrary, means an excess of resources allocated to less poor regions. For example, in the case of the ambitious $US100 million-a-year Vaso de Leche (Glass of Milk) Programme, which sought to benefit 3.3 million (mostly) children nationwide, the estimated loss to the government was about $US58.4 million due to leakage and under-coverage. A leakage level of 15.3 per cent (as of 2004) meant 8,503,060 untargeted beneficiaries of age 13–64 had been reached, while the under-coverage rate of 68.5 per cent implied that 3,930,510 poor children less than 14 years old were excluded (Vásquez 2004b). Similarly, in 2003, leakage in all social programmes focused mainly on children reached 3.9 million, and calculated on the basis of the annual costs of each ration, about $US267 million were lost.[3] This is the cost that the state would incur every year due to inefficacy and lack of targeting of important social programmes for children.

Figure 4.2 shows the objective and coverage population of four Peruvian social programmes as percentage of national population from 2001 to 2007 (Vaso de Leche— Glass of Milk, Comedor Popular—Soup Kitchens, Desayuno Escolar—School Breakfast and Seguro Integral de Salud— Health Insurance). These graphs show that the targeted and under-covered population has been decreasing with time. According to Monge, Vásquez and Winkelried, this reduction is related to the reduction of the poverty rate. It declined from 54.8 per cent in 2001 to 40.6 per cent in 2007 (Monge et al. 2009).

(% Population)

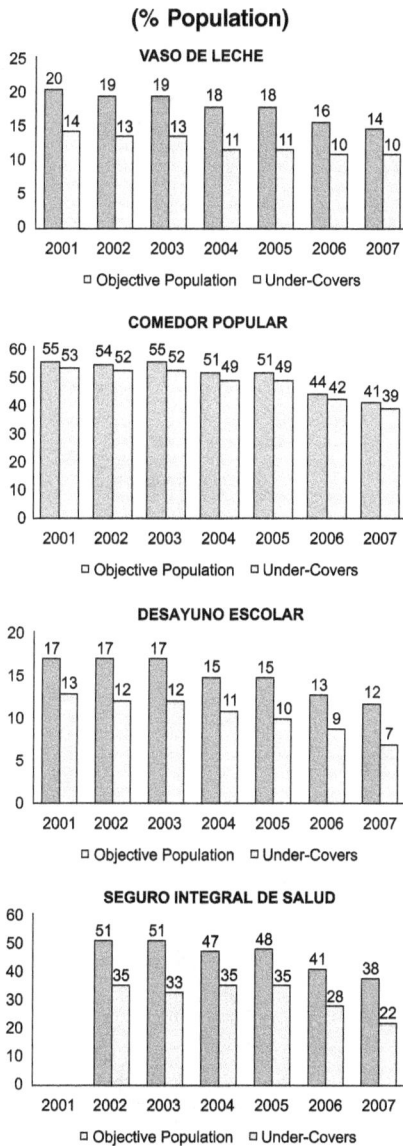

VASO DE LECHE

25, 20, 15, 10, 5, 0

20 19 19 18 18 16 14
14 13 13 11 11 10 10

2001 2002 2003 2004 2005 2006 2007

□ Objective Population   □ Under-Covers

COMEDOR POPULAR

60, 50, 40, 30, 20, 10, 0

55 53 54 52 55 52 51 49 51 49 44 42 41 39

2001 2002 2003 2004 2005 2006 2007

□ Objective Population   □ Under-Covers

DESAYUNO ESCOLAR

20, 15, 10, 5, 0

17 17 17 15 15 13 12
13 12 12 11 10 9 7

2001 2002 2003 2004 2005 2006 2007

□ Objective Population   □ Under-Covers

SEGURO INTEGRAL DE SALUD

60, 50, 40, 30, 20, 10, 0

51 51 47 48 41 38
35 33 35 35 28 22

2001 2002 2003 2004 2005 2006 2007

□ Objective Population   □ Under-Covers

Source: Enaho 2001 to 2007, fourth semester
Elaboration: Monge, Vásquez and Winkelried (2009).

Fig. 4.2: *Objective and Coverage of Population*

Figure 4.3 shows the number of participants and filtered population as the percentage of national population. The general tendency is that the change in the participation is accompanied with similar changes in the number of filtered (Monge et al. 2009).

(% Population)

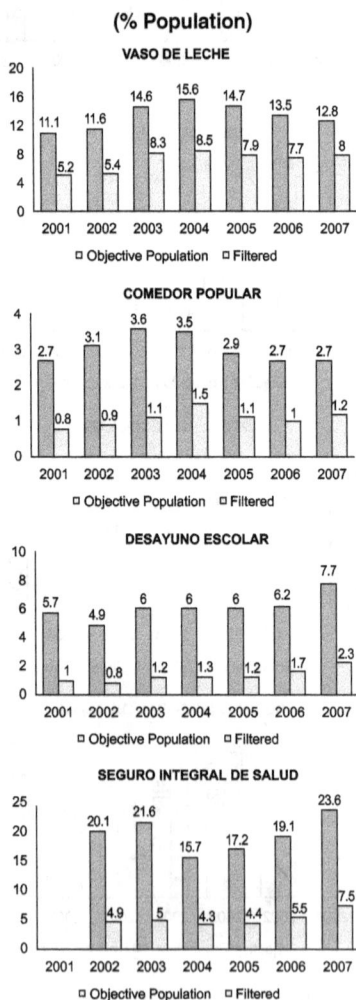

** Source: Enaho 2001 to 2007, fourth semester
Elaboration: Monge, Vasquez and Winkelried (2009).

Fig. 4.3: *Participants and Filtered Population*

Efficiency: Efficiency happens when a programme is implemented with average operative costs being kept as low as possible without compromising on the required quality and the possibility of improvements. Public works are often criticised for their administration and personnel cost, which diverts resources from the target population. So we suggest that efficiency standards for public firms or government be adopted from private firms, which do not spend more than 10 per cent of resources on these (Vásquez and Franco 2007).

Empirical evidence shows two main sources of inefficiency in social investment: incorrect focusing of programmes and budgetary allocations skewed towards administrative expenses. Most sectors have a high current component in spending, with salary payments—teacher, doctor, nutritional promoters and other salaries—taking away at least 90 per cent of budget allocations. For instance, in 2006, 70 per cent of the education sector's budget went into salary and pension payments. Some indicators to measure the optimality of public spending focused on children would be: (i) operative social investment per person in a programme, which will not include salaries, and how it has evolved, and (ii) proportion between the operative and administrative expenses of the programme.

Equity: This implies assigning resources to activities that help attain welfare with equal conditions and opportunities for all citizens. The problem of inequity has been persistent in Peru's social programmes. Resources for education, for instance, are not directed towards poorer areas. In Huancavelica, where 85.5 per cent of the people belong to the two poorest income quintiles spending per student in entry-level education was about $247.20, while it was $661.32 in Moquegua, with a smaller percentage of 29.8 per cent of people in those income categories (Vásquez 2005c).[4] An equitable distribution of spending in initial education would allow the inclusion of 43,518 children of 3 to 5 years of age from the regions with greater socioeconomic needs (ibid.).

The allocation of resources for initial education shows per capita spending of over a thousand soles (about 2.90 Nuevos Soles is equivalent to 1 US Dollar) for regions such as Moquegua and Tumbes, where less than 10 per cent do not have access to education, compared to less than 500 soles in regions of Huancavelica (467 soles) and Huánuco (310 soles) where over 90 per cent are so deficient. This regressive tendency prevails at all three levels of education (initial, primary, secondary and higher). This weakness present through the education chain, adversely impacts the child's potential entry into the job market. In the same way, if the allocated resources in the health sector were to be distributed evenly, 2,826,416 million poor would be covered, including 1,249,730 children (Vásquez 2005c). A progressive allocation of resources would have brought at least an additional 1.5 million children into the health and education programmes.

The inequity in the regions of Peru is related to the lack of development of technical and managerial capabilities, little orientation towards the achievement of goals and inertia of the current expenditure (Vásquez and Franco 2007). According to Vásquez (ibid.), the public spending in the eight richer departments or regions such as Lima, Tacna, Arequipa, Moquegua, Ica, Tumbes, Lambayeque and La Libertad is S/.670 higher than the amount for the poorer regions, Huancavelica, Huánuco, Cajamarca, Apurímac, Ayaucho, Loreto, Amazonas and Pasco (ibid.).

Transparency: This implies unlimited access for citizens to information to follow up on public management of resources. Specifically, it implies the ability to answer questions on how much, where and how public resources have been allocated and spent. According to Tesoro (2003), social control supported by transparency is the most effective, efficient and democratic way to evaluate the quality, effectiveness, efficiency and the equity of the allocation of the public budget (Vásquez 2006a: 45–80). Peru has begun the journey towards full transparency with the implementation of the Integral System of Financial Administration (SIAF) (ibid.).

Why an Information System is Vital

In most developing countries, there is no reliable information system that aids monitoring and public spending on children and supervising whether a state is truly committed to upholding children's rights. A methodology is required to allow public agencies to track social investment focused on children. One such is a system that monitors social programmes managed by municipal governments (Cuentas 2005) which allows decision-makers and the executive in municipal governments to have information, specifically about quality, that can be used in social management and to help strengthen the institutional evaluation capacities in favour of children (Vásquez 2006a).[5] These are tools to evaluate: (i) municipal social investment in children, (ii) how they have been implemented, and (iii) the quality of the management of those programmes. It also creates a permanent tracking instrument (Cuentas 2005).

According to Cuentas (2005), successful implementation should be based on six stages:

First: For selection of the programmes, the first step is to determine the importance the municipal government is giving to social programmes in its budget, or the percentage of resources allocated to social investment. Next, we pick the programmes that specifically target children to ascertain the importance of the target group within the total population covered by this municipality.

Second: Here, we focus on the elaboration and agreement of operative annual plans (POA) of the programmes for children.[6] A POA is a roadmap for a year's activities in a certain agency and gives the coverage goals for each programme and the resources needed to achieve them. The agreement of POAs is a step intended for community involvement.

Third: The evaluation of the social investment should be done via indicators such as the municipal income growth rate, children mortality rates and chronic malnutrition rates, among others.[7] Qualitative indicators can also be created to evaluate components that cannot be quantified.

It is necessary that every module has pertinent indicators. For example, while a relevant indicator for the institutional module would be 'proportion of municipal investment on children', it would be 'chronic malnutrition rates' for the execution aspect. The indicators also give us the dimension of the problems of a district, the starting point in the development of policy, programmes and projects to improve the situation. This stage is a vital process because it allows government agencies to monitor a programme. It is also important to establish the frequency of the information needed, the yardsticks of its measurement, and the branches of the municipality to generate it.

Fourth: For the system to run efficiently, responsibilities have to be assigned to each unit within the municipality for generating and processing information, constructing indicators, using and diffusing data adequately. It is also necessary to have a flow chart mapping the circulation of information, to know every step of the process as well as the units and thereby avoid duplication.

Fifth: This stage, with six modules, is the nucleus of the methodology, introducing other central aspects of public management such as transparency and equality. The system is divided into two groups. The first focuses on structure, organisation and institutional functioning; the second evaluates the system in both processes and input, or in other words, crucial feedback. The first group is divided into four modules, and the second two.

1. *Municipality Activities Module* gives information of the target population, the working environment, the annual budget, and the objectives of the programmes for children.

2. *Institutional Module* is a set of indicators for the social investment made by the municipality for children as well as for the programme beneficiaries.
3. *Alert Module* collects information about the problem that each of the programmes seeks to solve in a specific area, or in other words, indicators about the living standards of children. In that sense, it gives warning signals about the magnitude and depth of the problems.
4. *Result Module* provides a set of indicators to evaluate the municipality's social investment directed towards children as a whole and provides a benchmark for tracking its efficient use.
5. *Process Evaluation Module* contains indicators to evaluate the operation model of the social programmes with children as targets, for instance, if management of the programmes was efficient, degree of specialisation of the programmes, synergies established with other institutions to optimise results, systems to determine if children have graduated upwards from being beneficiaries, as well as the level of commitment of citizens and social organisations in management.

   To give an example of how this works, say, in the case of the specialisation indicator, we use the indicator 'resources allocated to children in the programme'. This is the percentage of expenditure made in activities related to children in relation to the total expenditure of the programme. Similarly, the 'graduation rate' can be constructed by calculating the percentage of children that left the programme, because they finished primary school or became well-nourished as the case may be, out of the total number of beneficiaries.
6. *Input Evaluation Module* is a set of indicators that give information about the quality of procedures in

the provision of the service, human resources in the programme, the systems of information that can be used, and monitor the relationship between the municipality and the citizens with the providers. Examples of such indicators would be 'expenditures to improve services' which is the share of the expenditure made in improving services out of the total expenses of the programme, or 'complaints attended by the programme'.

Sixth Stage: This should ensure diffusion of information in a user-friendly way in order to maintain a transparent environment of functioning. It can be done via a web page, informative bulletins for citizens, radial programmes, executive reports about the administration, and so on.

Peru urgently needs a legislative measure to establish a separate system of monitoring and evaluation for social programmes to ensure efficient and proper use of resources (Vásquez 2004b). Monitoring promotes a culture of transparency, encourages availability of information on beneficiaries and allows tracking of state commitments to children (ibid.).

To calculate socioeconomic indicators covering access to health services, education, nutrition, justice and welfare and analysing them, we use 'household living standard surveys', 'household surveys' and 'demographic and health surveys'. In the case of Peru, the National Household Survey (ENAHO) prepared by the Instituto Nacional de Estadística e Informática (INEI) in both rural and urban areas has been available since May 2003. In some cases, for the construction of indicators, the ENAHO presents direct questions that can facilitate calculation. For example, to determine the frequency of sickness among children, the question is, 'In the past weeks, have you had any disease?' and the answers given by the number of people below 18 that answered the question positively are useful (Vásquez 2005a). In some cases, cross-checking information or data is required, for instance, to determine the incidence of disease by spending levels and in regions.

Evaluating State's Compliance of Rights Commitments

Respect for children's rights must be made tangible by social spending, that is, allocations for children in public budgets for health, education, nutrition, justice and any other intervention that leads to improvement in child welfare. The starting point is access to information and a quality, standard database. A more exhaustive analysis would need a look at transparency and accountability of the public sector too.

But interpretation of data is beset with pitfalls. If social spending is considered as a percentage of GDP, and it jumps from 4 per cent to 9 per cent, this does not necessarily reflect more investment in social spending by the government; it can also mean a smaller GDP. Likewise, if spending in health falls the connotation may not necessarily be negative. It could even mean the opposite; that health spending is going down with improvement in health condition and efficiency of fiscal policy.[8] A state preoccupied by spending in health or education will allocate more resources to these sectors, even if the budget is constant or reduced; while another state that is unconcerned will allocate less resource even if its budget grows. Therefore, the right way to verify the importance of social spending in the budget is to analyse the variable of spending in health or education against the total spending.

From this, many interesting analyses could be developed. For example, the relationship between military expenditure (or M) to health or education spending (or S). This would give us the relative importance of the two in the state budget. If M/S is more than 2, we would find ourselves in an alarming situation where the state gives double the money to the army than to health or education needs.

Another analysis that could track state compliance with children's rights relates to devoting social expenditure to the less poor. We could track this and see if social spending is related to any variable that measures poverty. We also have to evaluate such expenditure in per person terms as some administrative divisions may be getting more money simply because they have more people.

Narrowing the gender gap in rural education: Evaluating State Compliance

The importance of education as a mechanism in bringing down poverty is undeniable. From a profitability perspective, Haveman and Wolfe (1984) show investments in education are more profitable than other types of investment, such as the acquisition of productive assets, state-owned entrepreneurship, etc. A study by Appleton (2000) on Africa's rural areas shows that increased schooling for children can have significant positive impacts on agricultural productivity.[9] Returns for complete primary education show over 10 per cent rise in agricultural productivity. And in the case of individuals who have completed secondary education, returns go up to 12 per cent as they tend to shift their work supply towards non-agricultural activities. Thus it is essential that children enter the labour market with the highest possible levels of education.

The World Bank (1999) highlights that education, besides raising productivity in individuals, also promotes better nutrition and health standards, empowerment of economic agents, and social cohesion. Studies also demonstrate the positive correlation between the education status of parents and the levels of human capital achieved by their children in terms of health and education. In developing countries there is a positive association between parents' educational level and improvements in children's weight and height (Ahn et al. 1995). Better educated parents re-examine education's role as a mechanism of welfare and future development and have more incentives to send children to school. Likewise, studies emphasise the overwhelming role of mothers in education and preventive health care.

Children of educated parents are more likely to be taken to the doctor and given all recommended vaccines against life-threatening diseases. At the end of 2001, 950,000 adults in rural areas of Peru had never attended school. Nearly 1.35 million over the age of 18 could not read or write. Women represented 76 per cent and 74 per cent of these numbers. In the same year, Law N° 27558 (*Ley de Fomento de la Educación de las Niñas and Adolescentes Rurales*) was passed in order to provide rural girl children with more education opportunities through resources and institutional development, and narrow the gender gap in education. Unfortunately, even after the law was passed, exclusion and poor quality of education for rural girl children continues. Almost 192,000 rural girl children (average school attendance rates are 15 per cent) in schooling age (6 to 16) are still out of school and about a million girl children, or 70 per cent of all between 7 and 17 years of age show a degree of educational backwardness (Vásquez and Monge 2007).

Figure 4.4 shows that the major gender gap is at the primary level. The proportion of boys registered in primary

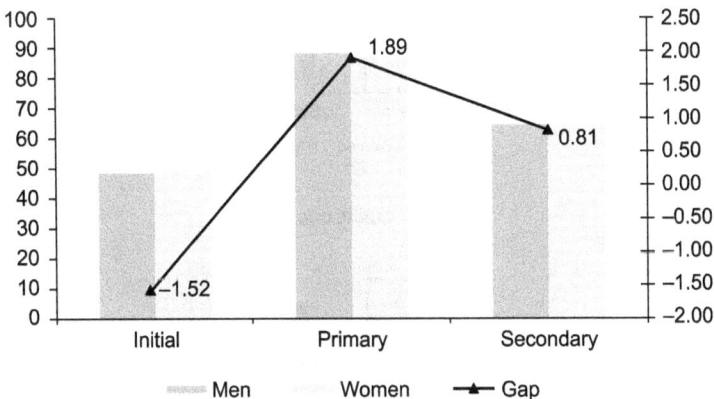

Source: INEI (2005c).
Elaboration: Centro de Investigación de la Universidad del Pacífico.

Fig. 4.4: *Net rate of school enrollment in basic education (by sex)*

education is 1.89 per cent greater than girls (Vásquez 2009). The principal reason for this is that girls' parents have a high opportunity cost to send them to school. Monge and Vásquez (2009) argue that this opportunity cost in rural areas is the dedication of girls to domestic work. They also point out that disparity increases the intergenerational transmission of poverty. A solution for this could be a system of conditional monetary transmission focused on rural girls.

In Peru, rural girls have less chances of access to an education than boys. Many girls enroll for primary level, but fail to complete it. The gap between girls and boys is wider in rural highlands than in the coast (see Figure 4.5). Thirty-one per cent of women had not started their primary education against 7 per cent of men and the proportion of women with some secondary level education is 17 per cent while in the case of men it is 34 per cent (Monge and Vásquez 2009).

According to geographic regions in 2007 (% population)

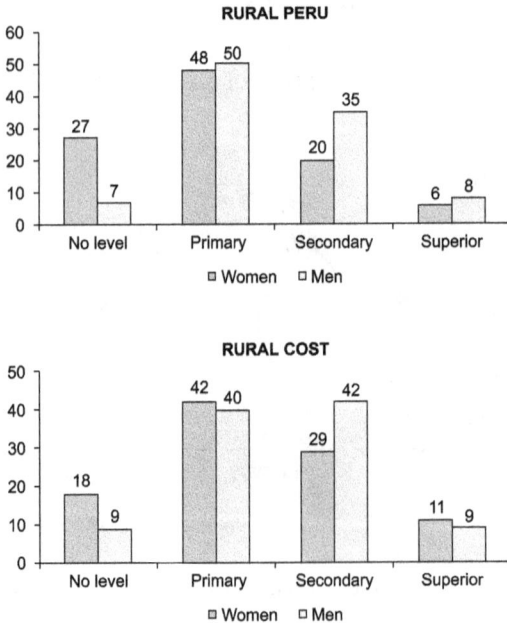

RURAL PERU

RURAL COST

RURAL HIGHLANDS

Women ☐ Men

RURAL JUNGLE

Women ☐ Men

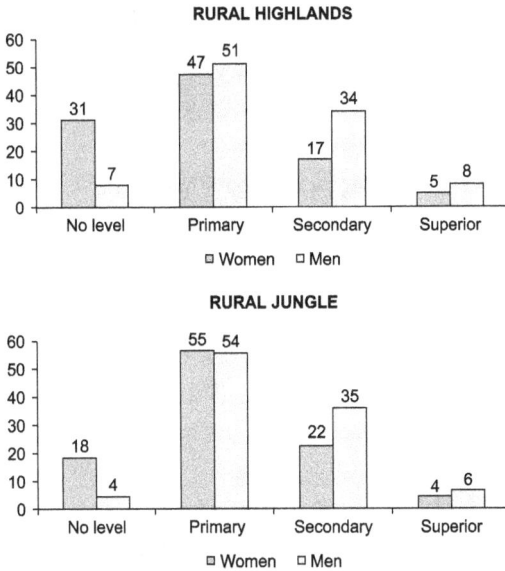

Source: INEI (2007). Encuesta Nacional de Hogares, 2007.
Elaboration: Monge and Vásquez (2009).

Fig. 4.5: *Educational Level reached for adult population*

Statistical evidence (Monge and Vásquez 2009) shows
that to develop education for boys and girls alike, Peru must
focus its efforts on the following:

• **Investment in Infrastructure:** The lack of minimal
infrastructure, such as roads or public conveyance or
nearby schools, implies transportation costs that
become a significant access barrier. In rural areas,
parents prefer having their girl children in charge of
the household or under their own care at home
because there is no transportation security. This
problem is widespread in initial and secondary
education levels, since only 20 per cent and 13 per
cent of rural townships report having transportation
infrastructure in these two areas respectively.

• **Health protection and insurance:** Protection in
terms of health care for rural children must be among

the state's priorities as close to 45 per cent of people do not have any type of insurance.[10] Girl children between 12 and 17 years especially are the vulnerable group in terms of health as 41 per cent of these have no insurance whatsoever.

- **Nutrition Programmes:** Malnutrition generates academic shortcomings, and more so, if the prevalent culture undermines girls' chances to attend school. The hardest step is the first, so strong motivation is needed to overcome these obstacles. The existence of nutritional programmes can provide that motivation.[11]

What principles should guide the design and execution of policies that encourage the girl children's enrolment and continuing in school? We consider the following factors useful.

- **Reduction of the cost of education:** Subsidies could reduce the cost of education for the target population. This can take the form of scholar gratuity in state-owned schools or partial or total scholarships in private schools. Subsidies could be awarded as scholarships for students who do well in studies or are gifted or belong to minorities. A very good way would be to give stipends linked to attendance so that the family's opportunity costs associated with sending children to school goes down, or pay for school materials like books, uniforms, etc.

- **Education for food programmes:** Such measures imply distribution of food rations to students to ensure and promote regular attendance. Food can either be distributed for in-school consumption or it can take the form of dehydrated take-home rations. In some cases, essential food items such as bottled cooking oil can also be given as incentives.

- **Making schooling a practical possibility:** Measures that seek to materialise the access of education, such as building enough schools, must be put into force.

Given the changing political and economic realities, it can also mean different things in different countries. In countries caught in conflict-situations, for instance, it means achieving a state of peace that allows children to attend schools regularly during conflict.

- **Making schools girl-friendly:** This is the least known measure but is essential to overcome beliefs in traditional households that encourage gender differences and discourage enrolment of girls. Such beliefs relate to prohibition of girl–boy interaction among the more orthodox practitioners of Islam or fear of sexual abuse. Often, the lack of separate hygienic services (simply, bathrooms with closing doors) can discourage school attendance, and hiring female teachers can encourage girls to join schools.
- **Improving the quality of education:** Such measures seek to raise the value of schooling so that it justifies incurring the costs associated with enrolment. Measures include allocating funds to hire more teachers or specialised teachers. It can also mean tailoring education to the needs of rural children. Improving educational quality means increasing the value of the services offered to the child and her parents.
- **Awareness Raising:** Awareness-raising programmes are measures not meant specifically as an action but to generate an indirect impact on the target population. Advocacy campaigns that promote empowerment of women have direct impacts on girl children's school enrolment rates. In the case of India, for example, the Mahila Samakhhya programme contributed to raising girls' enrolment.
- **Strengthening Educational Management agencies:** In some countries, resources are allocated to strengthen agencies that supervise the education system or strategic agencies that work to improve education levels.

- **Changing attitudes and upgrading skills:** If transparency and accountability are the main concern of citizens with regard to administration of public resources in each of the state agencies of the public sector and civil society, it is then essential to generate tools that contribute to changing attitudes and upgrade skills among citizens. The use of public assets must focus on efficiency, efficacy, equality and transparency. The adult population must be aware how much, how and on what public resources are spent—those resources which come largely from taxes paid by them. For these reasons, it is important to encourage parents' and even children's association with educational institutions, to allow them to acquire basic managerial skills. At a very early stage in their academic development, children must learn positive values in the administration of public resources, enriching their educational experiences.

Texts intended for teachers and students of both primary and secondary education on these subjects must be made available to familiarise them with concepts concerning the state, the economy, public spending and participative budgets with a focus on childhood.

In the case of Peru, two Participative Balanced Budget (PEP) manuals were published; one in APAFAs (Parents Association) (Save the Children Suecia and CEDISA 2005a), focused on aiding parents in preparing a budget that represents the interests of stakeholders, not excluding weaker groups. The second manual was published for school municipalities, seeking to promote direct student participation in school public matters as well as strengthening the student institution as a space for children to exercise citizenship. It also seeks to transmit transparency mechanisms and create a culture of accountability (Save the Children and CEDISA 2005b).

As a starting point, basic budget concepts must be clear. Concepts such as nation, state functions, levels of government and their basic functions must be understood. All responsibilities of every agency of government should be defined to avoid functional duplicity and inefficient use of resources.

As a first step within the guidelines for PEP, an Educational Institution's Strategic Plan must be prepared. This document is a management tool that allows a cohesive vision of the education institution and must seek to answer these questions:

(i) Mission: Who are we? What do we seek? How do we want to achieve our future goals?
(ii) Vision: What do we want to achieve? When will we achieve it?
(iii) Principles: Why do we do it?
(iv) Institutional Situation: What do we have? What can we do? Who can help us? What should we give priority to?
(v) Objectives: What can we do in this period?

The elaboration of a PEP must be based on four basic principles: efficiency, in terms of executing activities with low operative costs while maintaining adequate quality standards to ensure improvements; efficacy, in terms of reaching programme goals in the proposed timeframes while maintaining quality expectations from parents; transparency, in terms of providing free flow of information; and equality, so as to assign resources that give the same opportunity to all students to do well. It must be understood that not all classrooms or grades can be beneficiaries at the same time and priorities will have to be assigned to meet specific needs in terms of urgency. There must be consensus in that not all problems can be solved at once.

The PEP preparation procedure that is discussed within the organisational structure of the APAFA should use the following step-by-step method: (i) Teachers, as PEP promoters should provide information and answer questions from parents from the Classroom Committees, (ii) Discussion within each committee about the priorities of the educational institution based on the strategic plan, (iii) Discussion among Committee President's Assembly and definition of PEP elaboration rules, (iv) Discussion between the Directive Council and the Classroom Committee President Commission, (v) Presentation of PEP proposal to general assembly and acceptance or modifications, and (vi) Control and monitoring of PEP execution.

Within the organisational structure of school municipalities, the PEP process should be organised in the following steps:[12] (i) As in the case of APAFAs, teachers should be the first promoters of the process and inform and clear all doubts among students. (ii) The Student Council should define the rules for PEP elaboration. (iii) Classroom-level discussion on different themes such as education, culture and sports, etc. should be conducted and activities to prioritise in the institution as well as possible financing means discussed. (iv) Discussion in workgroup levels by themes according to prior classroom level discussions. (v) Workgroup representatives meeting and definition of investment and finance plan. The activities as well as financing mechanisms have to be discussed and implemented according to the school municipalities' capacities and their potentials. (vi) Control and monitoring of the execution of the investments and finance plan.

Conclusion

The efforts to evaluate the last eight years' public spending on children by the Peruvian government can be divided into three main groups.

First, a series of publications such as '¿Los niños . . . primero?: El gasto público social focalizado en niños y niñas en el Perú: 1990-2000', '¿Los niños . . . primero? Volume II Cuánto invirtió el Estado Peruano en los niños, niñas y adolescentes (2001–03)', '¿Los niños . . . primero? Volume III Niveles de vida gasto público social orientado a la infancia (2004–05)' give revealing statistics and exemplary cases relating to the lack of investment in education, health, nutrition, justice and welfare and lay bare the shortcomings of public budget management.

Second, it is well known that public agencies as well as private institutions in developing countries lack technical knowhow of public budgets and living standard surveys. Due to its limited diffusion, the approach of children's rights is not known among all social sectors. For this reason, the methodology presented in this essay, known as the *Metodologia de la Visualización de los niños y las niñas en los Presupuestos públicos del Perú*, was taken to municipal governments in Lima and San Martin as well as many federal government agencies with successful results. The publication of *Manuel Global: ¿Cómo investigar para que los niños sean primero en los presupuestos públicos en los países en desarrollo?* (Vásquez 2005a) is expected to become a vital tool in strengthening the monitoring of social spending aimed at children. Two tangible results can be mentioned. First is the formulation of indicators of results, processes and input for public spending in the provinces of Ica and the district of Jesus Maria. Second is the elaboration of a preliminary version of the paper *¿Los niños ... primero? El caso de Colombia* prepared by the Pontificia Universidad de Cali. Both results are a product of inter-institutional partnerships within guidelines programmed by Universidad del Pacífico and Save the Children Sweden.

Third, there has been the development of spaces for interaction to promote a culture of accountability and social vigilance regarding social spending for vulnerable groups within the Peruvian children. With the publication of texts about the state, economics, public spending and participative budgets, this knowledge has become accessible to teachers, APAFA members and students. Thus, we have contributed to changing the attitude towards the use of public resources in an efficient, effective, equitable and transparent manner.

Social spending has been increasing steadily since 1994 in real terms, rising from 4.3 per cent of GDP in 1994 to 9.31 per cent in 2004 (INEI). Still, the misery continues. Over half of Peruvians live in poverty; a quarter of children younger than 5 suffer from chronic malnutrition, a quarter of the population does not have access to health services and 54 per cent of students are still at zero (on a scale of 0–5) in the OECD Programme for International Student Assessment (PISA), an international evaluation of language.[13] To increase spending on children and public accountability, a congressional bill, called The National System of Monitoring and Evaluating Social Spending Focused on Vulnerable Infant Groups, on higher spending for children was presented in November 2006. It is currently with the Economy, Banking, Finances and Financial Intelligence Committee of Congress which must approve the bill.

ℐ

Notes

[1] All figures in US dollars.

[2] According to the conclusions and recommendations on the Children and Investment General Debate Day that took place in Geneva as a part of activities related to the Convention on Children's Rights.

[3] The following programmes were considered: Vaso de Leche, Seguro Integral de Salud, Comedores Populares, Desayunos escolares, Almuerzo Escolar and Comedor Infantil.

[4] A quintile is a fifth of a statiscal population sorted from lowest to highest on a specific feature.

[5] This manual collects the contributions of the suggested methodology prepared by Dr Enrique Vásquez which have been consolidated in his book *Metodología de visualización de los niños y las niñas en los presupuestos públicos del Perú*, for which many investigations took place in Lima and San Martin.

6 This makes reference to community involvement in municipal programming as well as the setting of resources for the said municipal actions.

7 Here the construction of indicators is focused on municipalities. More explanations in the next section.

8 This says governments should spend least when the economy is going through an expansive cycle.

9 Represents a four-year study.

10 That would be in the rural Andes, among adolescents aged 12 through 17.

11 World Food Programme (2001). School feeding works for girls' education.

12 In most educational institutions, the student council is organised into School Municipalities, comprising the mayor, the lieutenant mayor and councilmen for Education, Culture and Sport, Health and Environment, Children's Rights, Production and Services. It is democratically elected by the student body. Classroom Councils exist as well, with one mayor and four councilmen to each.

13 The Programme for International Student Assessment (PISA) is an internationally standardised assessment that was jointly developed by participating economies and administered to 15-year-olds in schools. Four assessments have so far been carried out (in 2000, 2003, 2006 and 2009). Data for the assessment which took place in 2009 was released on December 7, 2010. Tests are typically administered to between 4,500 and 10,000 students in each country.

𝔖

References

Ahn, Namkee and Abusaleh Shariff. 1995. 'Determinants of Child Height in Uganda: A Consideration of the Selection Bias Caused by Child Mortality', *Food and Nutrition Bulletin*, 16(1): 49–59.

Appleton, Simon. 2000. *Education and Health at the Household Level in Sub-Saharan Africa*, CID Working Paper No. 33, Center for International Development at Harvard University, USA.

Censo de 1993 and Censo Nacional de Talla en Escolares 1999. 'Nutrición y Retardo en el Crecimiento', Lima, Peru.

Cuentas, Martha E. 2005. *Cómo estamos invirtiendo en niñas and niños?* (Spanish), Save the Children Sweden (Suecia), Regional Program for Latin America and the Carribean, Peru.

El Instituto Nacional de Estadística e Informática (INEI). 2000. Encuesta Demográfica y de Salud Familiar, Lima, Peru.

———. 2005. Encuesta Demográfica y de Salud Familiar, Lima, Peru.

———. 2007. Encuesta Demográfica y de Salud Familiar, Lima, Peru.

Encuestas de Hogares Sobre Medición de Niveles de Vida (ENNIV) (English, National Survey on Living Standards). 2000. Análisis de Resultados, Dirección General de Censosy Encuestas, Lima, Peru.

Enquesta Nacional de Hogares (ENAHO) (English, National Household Survey). 2004. Instituto Nacional de Estadística e Informática, Lima, Peru.

Haveman, Robert and Barbara Wolfe. 1984. 'Schooling and Economic Well-being: The Role of Non-market Effects', Journal of Human Resources, 19(3): 377–407.

Instituto Cuanto. 2000. *Encuesta de Niveles de Vida 2000 (ENNIV 2000). Reporte Final*, October, Lima, Peru.

Monge, Alvaro and Enrique Vásquez. 2009. *Desigualdad de género en la educación de niñas y adolescentes rurales en el Perú: situación y propuestas de políticas públicas para su atención*, CIUP–Save the Children Suecia, Lima.

Monge, Alvaro, Enrique Vásquez and Diego Winkelried. 2009. '¿Es el gasto público en programmeas sociales regresivo en el Perú?' CIUP-CIES, Lima.

Save the Children Suecia and CEDISA. 2005a. *Presupuesto Equilibrado Participativo en las APAFA* (2005), Save the Children Suecia-CEDISA, Lima.

———. 2005b. *Presupuesto Equilibrado Participativo en Municipios Escolares* (2005), Save the Children Suecia-CEDISA, Lima.

Tesoro, José Luis. 2003. Portales pro-transparencia y transparencia de la anomia. Revista Probidad. No. 23–junio.

Vásquez, Enrique. 2004a. *Gasto social y niñez: las limitaciones de una gestión*, CIUP–Save the Children Suecia, Lima.

Vasquez, Enrique. 2004b. *Presupuesto Público y Gasto Social: La urgencia del monitoreo y evaluación*, CIUP–Save the Children Suecia, Lima.

———. 2004c. Los niños... primero? Volume II, Cuánto invirtió el Estado Peruano en los niños, niñas y adolescentes (2001–3), CIUP–Save the Children Suecia, Lima, Peru.

———. 2005a. *Manual Global por la Infancia. Cómo medir indicadores socioeconómicos y el gasto público social focalizado en niñas y niños de países en desarrollo*, CIUP–Save the Children Suecia, Lima.

———. 2005b. *Subsidios para los más pobres: ¿serán beneficiados los niños en extrema pobreza?* CIUP–Save the Children Suecia, Lima.

———. 2005c. *Presupuesto Público 2006: ¿A favor de la infancia?* CIUP–Save the Children Suecia, Lima.

———. 2005d. Los niños... primero? Volume III, Niveles de vida gasto público social orientado a la infancia (2004–5), CIUP–Save the Children Suecia, Lima, Peru.

———. 2006a. *La persistente brecha entre el discurso político y la gestión pública a favor de los más pobres. Un balance de los primeros 10 meses del segundo gobierno de Alan García*, CIUP–Save the Children Suecia, Lima.

———. 2006b. *Vulnerabilidad de las niñas y niños y el gasto social en la infancia en América Latina: ¿cómo hacer viable la vigilancia social por el cumplimiento de los derechos de la niñez?* in Niños, adolescentes, pobreza, marginalidad y violencia en América Latina y el Caribe: ¿relaciones indisociables?. Childwatch-International Research Network and CIESPI en convenio con la Pontifícia Universidade, Rio de Janiero, Brasil, pp. 45–80.

———. 2006c. Global Handbook for Childhood. How to Measure Socioeconomic Indicators and Child-targeted Public Spending in Developing Countries (Original title: *Manual Global por la Infancia-Cómo investigar para que los niños sean primero en los presupuestos públicos en los países en desarrollo?*), Save the Children Sweden Regional Program for Latin America and the Caribbean, Lima, Peru.

———. 2009. *Gerencia Estratégica de la inversión social*, CIUP–Save the Children Suecia, Lima.

Vásquez, Enrique and Álvaro Monge. 2007. *¿Por qué y cómo acortar la brecha de género en educación de las niñas and adolescentes rurales en el Perú?* CIUP–Save the Children Suecia–IPEDEHP–Manuela Ramos–ACDI, Lima.

Vásquez, Enrique and Enrique Mendizábal. 2003. Los niños... primero? El gasto público social focalizado en la niñez en Perú (1990–2000), Universidad del Pacífico, CIUP Save the Children Suecia, Lima, Peru.

Vásquez, Enrique and M. C. Franco. 2007. *Fusión de programas sociales en el Perú: Un fondo de inclusión social como propuesta*, CIUP–Save the Children Suecia, Lima.

Yamada, Gustavo. 2007. *Retornos a la educación superior en el mercado laboral: ¿Vale la pena el esfuerzo?* CIUP, Lima.

World Bank. 1999. The Education Sector Strategy, World Bank, Washington.

5

Pedagogy of Writing Disabled Children's Rights into Governance

Anita Ghai

'Childhood is the most intensively governed sector of personal existence . . . the focus of innumerable projects that purport to safeguard it from physical, sexual and moral danger, to ensure its "normal" development.'

> *A. James, C. Jenks and A. Prout, in* Theorizing Childhood
> *(Cambridge: Cambridge Polity Press, 1998)*

'We are not the sources of problems. We are the resources that are needed to solve them. We are not expenses, we are investments.'

> *Gabriela Arrieta of Bolivia and Audrey Cheynut of Monaco,*
> *May 8, 2002 in the opening address at the United Nations*
> *Special Session on Children, New York*

Introduction

Childhood is the most intensely governed sector of personal existence, implying that meaningful and significant changes should ensure normal development of children. Words such as 'child', 'children', 'citizen' and 'citizenship' have become a part of child rights vocabulary. The ways in which children negotiate, share and create with peers as well as adults reflect their socialisation process (Corsaro 1997). However, this active agency has not impacted one category of children, those who have heard more from adults than from children. They are the children with disabilities.

Despite being included in international human rights instruments, the UN Convention on the Rights of the Child as well as the latest United Nation's treaty on people with disabilities, there is very little hard evidence to show that disabled children occupy centre stage in decisions by the governments or are themselves key decision-makers. Life is tough for a child with a disability, and negotiating childhood and adolescence is a very complicated task. The lack of a responsive environment only makes life more difficult.

There are two very critical elements in the discussion on disabled children and issues of governance. First, the state's response in recognising the rights and entitlements of children with disability and second, the role played by the children themselves in decisions that concern them.

Definition: Who is a Disabled Child?

Disability can mean many things and cover quite a broad range of what is considered to be an impairment. Indeed, defining disability is not always simple. For instance, it covers people with intellectual, physical, sensory and psychiatric impairments. This complexity in what constitutes disability is translated into methods of data collection as well as authentic data on incidence of disability. In India, the census of 2001, for example, reports that there were 21,906,769 disabled people in January 2001 which is 2.13 per cent of the population. The number of disabled people within the age group 0–19 years, is 46,38,26,702 which is 1.67 per cent of the total population in the age group who are disabled (see Table 5.1). This data of disabled persons is marginally higher than the National Sample Survey Organisation's (NSSO) estimate of 18 million. The census commissioner of India believes that these results are more precise as the NSSO figures are only a rough estimate. As Mitra and Sambamoorthi (2006: 4024) conclude, 'prevalence estimates in the census and the NSSO are clearly not comparable . . . and it is unsure what aspects of disability are captured by the census and NSS current disability definitions'. That the government has not been unduly concerned about the figures is because they are not unduly concerned about persons with disability. This was reflected in the government's initial decision to exclude the disabled people from the 2001 census. The rationalisation was that the 1991 census revealed a very low incidence of disability, and therefore, did not warrant the creation of this category in the census of 2001. What was omitted from the discourse was the fact that the framing of disability in the 1991 census was done only in terms of a total incapacitation. This is a reflection of the attitude of the state towards disability because no individual, despite the severity of the impairment can be totally incapacitated (Ghai 2003). The 'definitional issues are at the heart of the differences between the estimates'. Jeffery and Singal (2008: 22) point out, 'Taking all disabilities together, the stricter definitions provide a lower estimate of 11.8 million people with disabilities while taking the wider definitions generates an estimate of 26.5 million'. Clearly, definition is at the very heart of planning. If there is lack of clarity on who constitutes 'disabled' the initiatives will be faulty too.

Children's growing up years are characterised by markers such as 'disabled', 'handicapped' and the more politically correct 'differently abled' and 'special'. In India the markers would include terminology such as *bechara bechari* (roughly translated into a patronising 'poor thing'); *langra/langri* (crippled), *andha* (visually impaired). Other countries would have their equivalent of these. Impairments may be temporary or permanent, requiring temporary or long-term measures.

Table 5.1: The disabled population within the age group
0–19 by type of disability, age and sex (Census 2001)

		Type of disability				
Total disabled population	21906769	In seeing	In speech	In hearing	In movement	Mental
		10634881	1640868	1261722	6105477	2263821
Disabled population in 0–19 age-group	7732196	3605553	775561	90452	2263941	796689
Disabled children as per cent of total population in 0–19 age-group	1.67%	0.78%	0.17%	0.01%	0.48%	0.17%
Disabled children as per cent of total disabled population	35.29%	33.9%	47.26%	23.02%	37.08%	35.19%

Source: Census of India 2001: Table C20 India.

To initiate the process of contending with disability is not an easy task. Though it appears that children are protected by a cohesive and constant familial network, in fact that is not so.

'Difference' brought about by impairment imposes on children a need to overcome limitations and hope for complete cure. It is a painful and disillusioning realisation to recognise that disabled children occupy a multifarious and marginalised position in Indian society, and indeed, in most other societies across the world, based on their disability and also on sociocultural identities that separate them into categories constructed according to such properties as caste (in South Asia and in some other countries), class, ethnicity and urban/rural divide. Indeed, disability is a deficiency that becomes a defining characteristic of the child, accounting mostly in terms of a 'medicalised' life history. Constituted as being profoundly 'Other', disability symbolically represents lack, tragic loss, dependency and abnormality. Because the possibility that human minds and bodies are always in transition, moving from an incomplete, imperfect and vulnerable existence, is not accorded to children, disability is an additional burden (Winnicot 1965). Exhibiting a structural amnesia that society displays, children who do not fit into the hegemonic discourse of 'normality' are excluded, separated and socially dis-empowered. A form of social and cultural apartheid, this seclusion is sustained by the creation of a built environment with amenities that solely cater to the needs of the more complete and able-bodied 'Other'. This social disregard coupled with experiences of social, economic and political subjugation deny the disabled children a voice, a space or even power to disrupt these deeply entrenched normative ideals that deprive them their social presence and any semblance of identity. While western literature has pro-gressed to analyse and understand disability as a social category, the same cannot be said of the research in India. By and large a reductionist stance has been adopted, in which disability is treated not as a life experience that needs to be understood in the context of relationships, but rather as a purely 'individual personal tragedy' that the disabled person needs to adjust to and come to terms with. The personal tragedy model posits a 'better dead than disabled' approach and reinforces the stereotype that the disabled cannot be happy, or enjoy an adequate quality of life. Within the larger Indian community, disability is understood as a punishment for past life sins by many. 'This theory implies that if one has committed misdeeds in previous births, one has to inevitably bear the consequences. Disability is held to be a punishment for the sins of previous births and one is called upon to accept it as divine retribution' (Dalal and

Pande 1999). Charity and philanthropy remain the predo-
minant responses to the predicament of disability in India,
without ever acknowledging the individual's own contri-
bution in the form of his/her bad deeds. Another strand of
this cultural construction conceives of disability as eternal
childhood, where survival is contingent upon constant care
and protection. Yet another strand considers disability as
a flaw and deficit. This attitude is deep rooted, and its traces
can be found in the traditional texts and scriptures and
even in social narratives such as the epic *Mahabharata*.
Thus in India the disabled are stigmatised as having a
deficient personality and the emphasis is on medical cure.
The social, economic and political aspects of disability
become secondary. Here, the emphasis is on images of
dependency, thereby reinforcing the charity/pity model. A
parent–child type interaction pattern characterises all social
relationships of the disabled (ibid.). The need for an interface
between childhood and disability can hardly be over-
emphasised. Disabled children have often been depicted as
passive, dependent and vulnerable; the voices of the children
themselves are strikingly missing from the discourse.
Contemporary society finds much in common between
childhood and disability as a category. This is evident in
the way both are socially produced and culturally
constructed. 'Children are considered "disabled" if they have
an identifiable level of "deficit" when formally measured or
compared with a social/cultural norm of learning, physical
abilities, etc. Like "disabled", children too are denied
attributions of agency, competence and civil rights' (Singh
and Ghai 2009: 130). Burns (1992) and Brown (1994) argued
that society, fearing the consequences in terms of
procreation wishes to keep people with 'disability' in a state
of 'suspended childhood'. In this view, children need to be
reared, raised, etc. if they are to become adults just like us,
if they are to support the world we've made, if they are to
'outgrow' or 'get over' their childish behaviour (Waksler
1991: 64).

Given this context wherein the disabled are coded as dependent, it is not surprising that disabled children's ideas to govern themselves have elicited indifference. This is not only because of the way the rest of the society views disability and is reflected in the state's response, but also because society's ideas and assumptions about disability are evoked and acted upon by the disabled children themselves.

State's and Society's Response to Needs and Rights of Disabled Children

Contemporary society's responses to childhood and disability (across age) as categories have much in common, because both are socially produced and culturally constructed. Children are not accorded agency because of their age and the disabled because of their condition. While it is assumed that children need to be dependent on adults on all matters that concern them and they are incapable of deciding what is right and good for them, the disabled persons are given a somewhat similar treatment. A disabled child is therefore doubly burdened with notions that govern attitudes and actions that are directed towards both. Children are considered disabled if they have an identifiable level of 'deficit' when formally measured or against comparison to a social/cultural norm of learning, physical abilities, etc.; like the disabled, children too are denied attributions of agency, competence and civil rights. They are both subject to mechanisms of control and surveillance exercised by the more powerful and 'normal' adults.

However, the reality is that notwithstanding the marginalisation and subjugation, disabled children do appear to have agency and decide about their fate. As one child with disability puts it, 'If you've got something to say, you've got something to say, it does not matter how young you are'.[1] A young disabled child said quoting a popular

Hindi song, *'Itni shakti hame dena mata, man ka vishwas kamjoor ho na'* (Give me so much strength that I do not lose faith). Whatever their impairment, disabled children can be skilled participants in everyday decision-making processes when they are provided with fair opportunities to interact both with other children as well as parents (Khanna and Ghai 2005). Presuming that 'disabled' children have a unitary identity as 'disabled', leads to a denial of other significant aspects of their experience. Davis and Watson (2001) and Khanna and Ghai (2005) indicate how 'disabled' children encounter discourses of 'normality' and 'difference' in school, arising from institutional factors and everyday cultural practices. A 'deficit thinking surrounds disabled people' (Goodley 2007: 319). Thus, 'disabled' children need to be understood as social actors, as controllers and as negotiating their complex identities within a disabling environment. The expectation of adults is that their experiential terrain is more relevant and children do not know the actuality. Some responses of state and society have been formulated as questions discussed in the following sections. The first question which is important is the personhood of the child.

The Search for Identity

Over the years the word 'disabled' has been replaced with what have come to be accepted as politically correct words such as children (persons) with special needs, differently abled children (persons); physically challenged or mentally challenged, etc. But has the change in nomenclature led to a change in the self-perception of the disabled of themselves and, also a change in attitude and action towards the disabled? Has the government become more inclusive in its programming? Has it enhanced the participation of the disabled in their role as citizens? Though some shifts are visible, neither has the self-perception of the disabled